Self-Love Ideas & Workbook

The Mindful Guide to Self-Worth and the
Positive Pillars of Healing; Self-
Appreciation, Forgiveness, Compassion
and Self-Worth

Nicholas Bright

any other individual or persons for any purpose other than that for which it was initially intended. It is strictly prohibited to amend, reproduce, distribute, utilize, quote, or paraphrase any part of the content within this publication without prior authorization from the writer or publisher. Any violation of these regulations may result in legal action against those who have breached them.

Disclaimer Notice

The presented work is strictly informational and should not be interpreted as an offer to buy or sell any form of security, instrument, or investment vehicle. Furthermore, the information contained herein should not be taken as a medical, legal, tax, accounting, or investment recommendation given by the author(s) or any affiliated company, employees, or paid contributors. In other words, the information is presented without considering individual preferences for specific investments regarding risk parameters. General information does not account for a person's lifestyle and financial objectives. It is important to note that no tailored advice will be provided based on the given information.

Table of Contents

CHAPTER 6: BUILDING YOUR SELF-LOVE TOOLKIT: COMPASSION, ACCEPTANCE, AND PRESENCE..81

CHAPTER 7: DAILY PRACTICES FOR A LOVING MINDSET: AFFIRMATIONS, JOURNALING, AND MINDFULNESS...94

CHAPTER 10: THE LIFELONG COMMITMENT: NURTURING SELF-LOVE EVERY DAY 133

CHAPTER 11: CUSTOMIZING YOUR SELF-LOVE PLAN: A TAILORED APPROACH 143

CHAPTER 12: DISPELLING MYTHS:

Welcome to the

Ideas Worth Sharing

Series

My name is Nicholas Bright, and I've spent nearly two decades working as a psychologist specializing in Behavioral Neuroscience and Interpersonal Communication in the US, UK, and Australia. Throughout my career, I've encountered countless stories, experiences, and insights that have shaped my understanding of the human mind and interpersonal interactions.

This series is a collaborative effort, bringing together the experience and expertise of myself and my colleagues: Erica May, Jeff Sharpe, Camila Alvarez, and potentially new faces in the future! We've chosen to write under pen names to respect everyone's privacy and keep the spotlight on the valuable content we offer rather than us as individuals. This decision allows us to freely share our knowledge without the distractions that often come with the limelight. We stand by the authenticity and credibility of the content shared here—our professional integrity remains at the forefront of this series.

We are deeply passionate about our field, and our primary goal is to equip you with practical, research-backed insights that you can implement in your everyday life. Each chapter is designed to inspire and help you better understand yourself and those around you.

We invite you to engage actively with the material: take notes, discuss the ideas with friends and family, and, most importantly, apply the lessons in your daily routine.

1. **Read;** understand what can be done to improve
2. **Reflect;** appreciate your feelings and their origins
3. **Remember;** put your learning into action

Thank you for embarking on this journey of knowledge and growth with us,

Nick

Want to Win Free Books?

Join Our Newsletter!

In this series, we appreciate that someone may find many different books helpful. I certainly know that when discussing sensitive topics like, for example, divorce, we can end up working on grief, anxiety, self-confidence, cognitive dissonance, and lots more. When we encounter a major challenge in life, it is rarely due to one small problem but rather a concoction of our experiences, outlooks, and actions; it's often a deep-rooted issue with many different things we need to uncover and support. We are complicated beings, and we must recognize this. As such, I would love to invite you all to join our newsletter.

In this, I aim to write articles of interest, including excerpts from various books in the series, as well as **vouchers**, **discounts**, and **giveaways**—and of course, no gimmicks or catches. I harbor a deep loathing of companies that offer seemingly amazing deals, only to charge you vast amounts in hidden fees! I vowed to never fall into that trap myself, and any offers I make are designed to be of true benefit and help. If you win a book in a giveaway, I want you to read it with a smile.

Join our newsletter and discover the additional value we can add to your life's curriculum!

Join us at: **www.IdeasWorthSharingSeries.com/newsletter**

See you on the inside!

About the Author: Dr. Nicholas Bright

Dr Nicholas Bright, a highly esteemed Clinical Psychologist based in the vibrant city of New York, is devoted to preventing and treating mental health problems. Nicholas earned his Clinical Psychology degree from Syracuse University, nestled in the heart of New York State. His practice is centred around mindfulness-based therapies, humanistic approaches, and positive psychology principles, enabling individuals to discover their potential and build emotional and psychological resilience.

He has maintained professional ties and a personal friendship with Erica May since their university years. Together, in the Ideas Worth Sharing series, they aim to extend their therapeutic expertise beyond their clinical settings through a series of books on critical psychological topics. This series will delve into various mental health themes, offering comprehensive advice on integrating emotional balance and humanistic practices into everyday life and techniques for fostering positive mental health.

By sharing practical examples and insights from his clinical work, Nick intends to make evidence-based psychological concepts accessible to the general public. His ultimate goal is to empower individuals with the knowledge and tools to manage their mental health effectively, enhance overall well-being, and build resilience.

Preface

"To love oneself is the beginning

of a lifelong romance."

Oscar Wilde

As I pen this preface, Oscar Wilde's words echo with profound clarity, capturing the essence of the transformative journey we will embark upon together. This book is a heartfelt exploration of self-acceptance, self-love, and the liberating power of overcoming self-doubt. Each page is crafted to guide you, the reader, through practical and actionable steps towards nurturing a loving relationship with yourself, even amidst a hectic life that seems to leave little room for personal reflection.

The inspiration to write this book stemmed from countless conversations with individuals who, much like you, have been ensnared by the tendrils of societal expectations and self-imposed pressures. The common thread in these interactions was the pervasive sense of not being enough—of constantly striving yet perpetually failing to meet both external standards and internal aspirations.

This book draws upon various sources for its foundational ideas—ranging from psychological theories and mindfulness practices to real-life anecdotes like those of Sarah and James. Each chapter builds on the last, designed to slowly but surely replace your critical self-talk with a compassionate inner voice.

A special note of gratitude goes to my mentor, Dr. Lisa Feldman, whose insights into emotional health have significantly shaped this work and to my family, whose unwavering support made this book possible.

As you turn these pages, remember that you are investing time in yourself—a worthy endeavour that reaps immeasurable rewards. You are not alone in your feelings or experiences, and it is not selfish to prioritize your well-being; it is necessary.

If you are ready to challenge old narratives and embrace new, empowering truths about yourself, this book is for you. It assumes no prior knowledge of psychology or self-help methodologies—only a willingness to explore your inner world and embrace change.

Thank you for choosing to embark on this journey with me. I invite you now to continue reading, engage actively with the exercises provided, and allow yourself to arrive at the profound love you so richly deserve. Let's begin this journey together towards building resilience, enhancing mental health, and ultimately discovering **the love you deserve**.

Introduction

"Forgiveness is not always easy. At times, it feels more

painful than the wound we suffered to forgive

the one that inflicted it. And yet, there is no

peace without forgiveness."

Marianne Williamson

In a world where the clamour of criticism, both internal and external, threatens to undermine our inherent worth, the pursuit of self-love emerges as a vital beacon of hope. This book is born from the recognition that amidst the chaos and the relentless pace of modern life, finding and holding onto self-love is not just beneficial; it's essential. It aims to guide you through the tumultuous waters of self-doubt and into the serene harbours of self-acceptance, equipping you with the necessary tools to build a foundation of love that emanates from within.

At the heart of this narrative is the profound understanding that self-love is not a destination but a journey—a continuous process of discovery, acceptance, and growth. The chapters that unfold serve as milestones on this transformative path, each offering unique insights and practical strategies rooted in the principles of mindfulness, compassion, and positive psychology. Through vivid explorations and exercises, you're invited to engage deeply with your inner self, confront your critical voice, and cultivate a relationship with yourself that is kind, forgiving, and supportive.

One of the core tenets of this book is the recognition that our thoughts and beliefs about ourselves shape our reality. It endeavours to unravel the complex web of negative self-talk, shedding light on how these patterns are formed and how they can be dismantled. By challenging and replacing these beliefs with affirmative, truth-based narratives, you're encouraged to rewrite your story with compassion at its core.

The narrative also broaches the significant yet often overlooked aspect of setting healthy boundaries—physical, emotional, and mental. It underscores how boundaries are not barriers but expressions of self-respect and acts of self-love. Through practical advice and real-life examples, you'll learn how to establish and maintain boundaries that honour your well-being and support your personal growth.

In addition to exploring the inner landscape of self-perception, this book acknowledges the external influences that shape our self-view, including relationships, culture, and social media. It provides strategies for navigating these influences mindfully, ensuring that the pursuit of self-love remains grounded in authenticity and personal truth.

Mindfulness is another pillar of this guide, presented not as a fleeting trend but as a fundamental practice for fostering self-awareness and presence. By cultivating mindfulness, you can connect with the present moment, recognize your thoughts and feelings without judgment, and nurture peace and contentment within yourself.

Affirmations—positive, empowering statements that counteract negativity and bolster self-confidence—are also explored as powerful tools for building self-love. This book includes a curated selection of affirmations designed to resonate with diverse experiences and challenges, offering a resource you can turn to whenever you need a reminder of your worth.

Self-care, often miscast as mere indulgence, is reclaimed here as an act of radical self-love. The text provides a framework for understanding self-care in its truest sense—caring for your physical, emotional, and spiritual well-being—and offers suggestions for integrating self-care practices into everyday life.

Lastly, this guide acknowledges the cyclical nature of self-love, recognizing that setbacks and advances are all part of the process. It emphasizes the importance of resilience, the grace of self-compassion, and the strength that comes from community and connection. It's about loving yourself in solitude and how self-love allows you to show up in the world—more compassionate, authentic, and connected to others.

This book does not offer a quick fix or a one-size-fits-all solution. Instead, it presents a path—a sometimes challenging, often rewarding—towards self-love that beckons with the promise of a more fulfilling and self-compassionate life. Through these pages, you are invited to step into your power, armed with the knowledge and practices that foster an unshakeable foundation of love for yourself.

Chapter 1: Beyond the Hustle: Discovering Self-Love Amidst Chaos

"Owning our story and loving ourselves through

that process is the bravest thing that

we will ever do."

Brené Brown

Is Self-Love Really Possible in the Chaos of Everyday Life?

Finding moments for self-reflection and care can seem not just luxurious but nearly impossible in a world that never stops bustling. The concept of self-love often gets lost amidst the chaos of deadlines, responsibilities, and societal expectations, especially for those in their late 20s to 40s. This pivotal age range is not only about career growth or family building but also involves deep personal development that frequently takes a backseat.

Understanding the impact of societal pressures and incessant busyness is crucial. It's easy to overlook how these external factors constantly shape our self-perception and behaviours. The hustle of everyday life doesn't just consume time and exhausts mental and emotional reserves, leaving little energy for personal nourishment. Recognizing this can be the first step in reclaiming the space needed for self-care and self-love.

Self-love is far from a mere indulgence; it is a fundamental necessity for well-being. Without it, our capacity to thrive and meet life's challenges diminishes. It strengthens resilience, enhances decision-making, and improves our relationships with others. By redefining self-love as essential, we prioritize it not as an optional add-on to our lives but as integral to our health.

For many, personal barriers such as guilt, time constraints, and deeply ingrained habits of prioritizing others' needs significantly hinder self-care practices. Identifying these barriers is a step towards dismantling them. It involves auditing one's daily routine, understanding where time is spent, and making conscious adjustments to embed acts of self-love throughout the day.

Practical strategies are pivotal in this journey towards embracing self-worth amidst daily tumults. Simple actions like setting boundaries, scheduling 'me-time,' or even turning mundane activities into moments of mindfulness can be transformative. These practices do not require sweeping changes but rather small, consistent acts that collectively lead to substantial outcomes.

Moreover, engaging in self-compassion is a powerful antidote to the harsh self-criticism many harbour. This entails treating oneself with the kindness one would offer a friend in distress. It's about acknowledging personal struggles without judgment and offering comfort and encouragement instead of criticism.

Transforming self-doubt into self-acceptance involves recognizing one's inherent worth despite imperfections or mistakes. It's about shifting focus from what you are not to appreciating who you are. This book aims to guide you through this transformation by providing tools that nurture self-compassion, encourage healthy self-care practices, and build resilience against external criticisms.

By committing to this path, you will cultivate a deeper love for yourself and create a life that reflects your true worth. The journey of self-acceptance is challenging and rewarding, offering profound benefits that extend beyond oneself into every facet of life.

Amid bustling schedules and societal expectations, it's easy to lose sight of the importance of self-love and self-care. The constant demands of daily life can overshadow our needs, leaving us feeling depleted and disconnected from ourselves. The pressure to excel in various roles, whether at work, at home or in relationships, often takes precedence over nurturing our well-being. It's a common struggle for many individuals, particularly those in their late 20s to 40s, who find themselves juggling multiple responsibilities while trying to meet external expectations.

Societal pressures play a significant role in undermining our sense of self-worth and self-love. The relentless pursuit of perfection fueled by social media, comparison culture, and unrealistic standards set by society can lead to feelings of inadequacy and unworthiness. We are bombarded with images of supposed "perfect" lives, bodies, and achievements, which can distort our perception of reality and fuel self-doubt. This constant exposure to curated versions of others' lives can erode our confidence and make us question our value.

Busy lifestyles further compound the challenge. The never-ending to-do lists, back-to-back meetings, family obligations, and social commitments leave little time for introspection or self-care. In the hustle and bustle of daily life, taking a moment to prioritize ourselves can feel like an indulgence we cannot afford. The idea of slowing down or taking time for self-nurturing activities may seem like a luxury reserved for those with ample free time – a notion perpetuating the cycle of neglecting our needs.

Recognizing these societal pressures and the impact of busy lifestyles is the first step toward reclaiming our sense of self-love. Understanding that we are not alone in facing these challenges can be empowering. Acknowledging that prioritizing ourselves is not selfish but necessary for overall well-being is essential. By unravelling the layers of external expectations and internalized pressures, we can see ourselves more clearly and cultivate a more profound sense of self-compassion.

Embracing Self-Love Amidst Chaos Requires a Shift in Perspective and Intentional Actions Toward Prioritizing Our Well-Being

Self-love is often misconstrued as a self-indulgent luxury reserved for those with abundant time and resources. However, self-love is not a privilege but a fundamental necessity for overall well-being. Prioritizing self-love is not selfish; it is essential for maintaining mental, emotional, and physical health. Neglecting self-love can lead to burnout, increased stress levels, and a diminished sense of self-worth.

Acknowledging the importance of self-love is the first step towards cultivating a more compassionate relationship with oneself. It involves recognizing your inherent value and treating yourself with the same kindness and respect you would offer others. Self-love is about setting boundaries, practicing self-care rituals, and nurturing emotional needs. By embracing self-love as a non-negotiable aspect of daily life, you pave the way for enhanced resilience and inner peace.

Embracing self-love requires a shift in mindset, viewing it not as an indulgence but as a vital component of a balanced and fulfilling existence. It involves dispelling the notion that putting oneself first equates to selfishness. Self-love empowers you to show up fully in all areas of your life, from personal relationships to professional endeavours. By recognizing your worth and honouring your needs, you create a solid foundation for emotional well-being.

Practical strategies can help integrate self-love into your daily routine. Simple acts of self-care, such as taking time for reflection, engaging in activities that bring joy, or setting boundaries to protect your energy, can make a significant difference in how you perceive yourself and navigate the world around you. Small changes can lead to profound shifts in mindset and overall outlook.

Remember that self-love is not a destination but a continuous journey. It requires consistent effort and commitment to prioritize your well-being amidst the chaos of everyday life. By intentionally honouring your needs, you demonstrate compassion towards yourself and set the stage for personal growth and fulfilment. Self-love is not an option but a cornerstone of leading a meaningful and balanced life.

Incorporating self-love into your daily routine may seem daunting, especially when faced with multiple responsibilities and external pressures. However, by reframing self-love as an essential component of overall wellness, you empower yourself to navigate life's challenges with grace and resilience. Start small, be gentle with yourself, and remember that every step taken towards embracing self-love brings you closer to living authentically and joyfully.

In the midst of daily responsibilities and external expectations, it's easy to overlook the importance of self-love. The constant demands of work, family, and social obligations can leave little room for prioritizing our well-being. However, recognizing and addressing personal barriers to self-love is crucial for cultivating inner peace and fulfilment. Let's delve into some common obstacles that may hinder our journey toward self-love and explore practical strategies to overcome them.

1. **Self-Criticism**: One significant barrier to self-love is the habit of self-criticism. Constantly berating ourselves for perceived flaws or mistakes can erode our self-worth and diminish our ability to practice self-compassion. To combat self-criticism, start by challenging negative thoughts with evidence-based affirmations. Remind yourself of your strengths and accomplishments, and treat yourself with the kindness you would offer a friend facing similar challenges.

2. **Comparison**: In today's hyper-connected world, it's all too easy to fall into the trap of comparison. Scrolling

through social media feeds filled with curated images of success and happiness can lead to feelings of inadequacy and unworthiness. Focus on your journey and accomplishments to break free from the comparison trap. Celebrate your unique qualities and achievements, recognizing that everyone's path is different and valid in its own right.

3. **Lack of Boundaries**: Setting boundaries is essential for protecting our mental and emotional well-being. Without clear boundaries, we may overextend our time and energy, leaving little room for self-care and reflection. Establishing healthy boundaries involves learning to say no when necessary, prioritizing your needs, and communicating openly with others about your limits.

4. **Perfectionism:** Striving for perfection can be a significant impediment to self-love. The relentless pursuit of flawlessness can lead to feelings of inadequacy and self-doubt, preventing us from embracing our imperfections with grace. Embracing imperfection allows us to cultivate self-acceptance and recognize that our worth is not contingent on achieving unattainable standards.

5. **External Validation:** Seeking validation from external sources, such as approval from others or societal norms,

can undermine our sense of self-worth. Relying on external validation for validation can be a slippery slope towards insecurity and low self-esteem. Practice validating yourself and acknowledging your worth independent of external opinions or expectations.

By identifying these personal barriers to self-love and implementing practical strategies to overcome them, we can pave the way for a more compassionate relationship with ourselves. Remember, self-love is not selfish but essential for overall well-being. Start by nurturing a kinder inner dialogue, setting healthy boundaries, and celebrating your uniqueness without comparison to others. Your journey towards unshakable self-love begins with recognizing your worth and taking intentional steps towards embracing it fully each day.

In the whirlwind of responsibilities and expectations that define modern life, self-love often falls by the wayside. Yet, as we've explored, this isn't merely a luxury; it's a **fundamental necessity** for well-being. Grasping this truth is the first step toward transforming how you view and treat yourself amidst daily chaos.

You might feel there's no space in your schedule for self-care, but I assure you that small, consistent actions can lead to substantial changes. The strategies outlined here are designed to be integrated into your busy life, ensuring that self-love becomes a seamless part of your everyday routine rather than another daunting task on your to-do list.

By recognizing the pressures placed upon us—both from within and without—we start to see the barriers to self-love not as insurmountable walls but as hurdles that can be overcome with persistence and the proper techniques. Embracing this mindset is crucial; it empowers you to reclaim your worth and prioritize your well-being, no matter how packed your agenda may seem.

As we move forward in this journey together, remember that every step you take is toward a more fulfilled and resilient self. The path to *unshakable self-love* involves continual learning and practice, but the rewards are immense. Not only will you feel better about yourself, but your enhanced self-regard will also radiate outward, positively affecting all areas of your life.

So, let's continue to break down these barriers. Let's make room for you in your own life. The transformation from self-doubt to self-acceptance is not just possible—it's within your reach, starting right now. Let each page of this journey equip you with everything you need to foster and maintain an enduring love for yourself.

Chapter 2: From Self-Sacrifice to Self-Nurturing: Shifting Mindsets

"Self-love, my liege, is not so vile a sin

as self-neglecting."

William Shakespeare, Henry V

Are You Truly Nurturing Yourself or Just Checking the Boxes?

Self-love is an essential foundation for a fulfilling life, yet many confuse it with mere self-care activities like spa days or indulgent treats. This chapter delves deep into the essence of self-love, which transcends these superficial acts and taps into a profound appreciation and respect for oneself. It's about recognizing your inherent worth and treating yourself with the same compassion and priority you often reserve only for others.

Self-love means moving from self-sacrifice to self-nurturing, a transition that requires a change in actions and a profound shift in mindset. For many, putting others first has become a deeply ingrained habit shaped by cultural norms and personal expectations. However, consistently placing others' needs aside can lead to burnout and resentment. It's crucial to understand that loving oneself isn't selfish; it's necessary.

To embark on this journey of self-nurturing, we must first differentiate between superficial self-care and genuine self-love. Superficial self-care often focuses on temporary relief or fleeting pleasures that do not address deeper emotional or psychological needs. In contrast, meaningful self-love involves engaging in practices that promote long-term well-being and growth. This includes recognizing when you're overextended and allowing yourself to step back and recharge without feeling guilty.

Acknowledging personal needs is another critical step in cultivating self-love. It begins with tuning into your body and mind to recognize what you truly need: rest, social interaction, or solitude. Setting healthy boundaries is equally important; it involves saying no when necessary, asking for help when overwhelmed, and not compromising your values or well-being to please others.

Treating oneself with kindness should be a daily practice, not an occasional treat. This means being as understanding and forgiving towards yourself as you would be towards a close friend. Prioritizing your well-being involves integrating habits that nurture both your physical health—like regular exercise and nutritious eating—and your mental health, such as mindfulness practices or therapy.

Implementing these changes may seem daunting, especially if you're used to neglecting your own needs. Start small: choose one aspect of self-nurturing to focus on each week. Whether setting aside time for meditation, scheduling regular check-ins to assess your well-being, or simply allowing yourself some downtime, each small step will lead you closer to embracing full self-love.

Remember, the journey toward self-love is ongoing and evolving. There will be days when you falter, and that's okay. The key is to persistently remind yourself of your worth and return to practices reinforcing this belief.

By shifting from self-sacrifice to self-nurturing, you enhance your own life and enrich the lives of those around you. A well-nurtured self can contribute more positively and sustainably in relationships and communities. Embrace this transformative journey with patience and persistence, knowing each step forward is a step towards the love you truly deserve.

Self-love is often associated with self-care, but the distinction between superficial self-care and deep, meaningful self-love is crucial. Superficial self-care involves surface-level activities like indulging in a bubble bath or buying oneself a treat. While these actions can temporarily relieve, they do not address the underlying need for self-compassion and genuine self-worth. True self-love goes beyond these fleeting moments of pleasure; it involves recognizing one's inherent value, treating oneself with kindness, and prioritizing well-being without guilt.

Deep self-love requires a shift in mindset from viewing self-care as a luxury to understanding it as a necessity for overall well-being. It entails acknowledging personal needs and setting boundaries that honour those needs. This shift can be challenging, especially for individuals accustomed to putting others' needs before theirs. However, embracing self-love means recognizing that prioritizing oneself is not selfish but essential for sustainable happiness and fulfilment.

Self-love is about nurturing oneself profoundly and addressing emotional, mental, and physical needs with compassion and care. It involves practicing self-compassion by speaking to oneself kindly, forgiving mistakes, and embracing imperfections as part of what makes each person unique. Individuals can navigate life's challenges with resilience and grace by cultivating this deep sense of self-worth.

In the journey toward self-love, moving beyond quick fixes and temporary pleasures toward practices that foster long-term well-being is essential. This may involve engaging in activities promoting inner peace and emotional balance, such as meditation, journaling, or leisure time in nature. Individuals can cultivate a lasting sense of fulfilment and contentment by investing in activities that nourish the soul and foster personal growth.

The transition from superficial self-care to deep self-love requires a conscious effort to prioritize one's well-being consistently. It involves recognizing when boundaries are being crossed and advocating for oneself with respect and assertiveness. By valuing oneself enough to set healthy boundaries and make self-care a non-negotiable part of daily life, individuals can lay the foundation for a more fulfilling and authentic existence.

Embracing Deep Self-Love Means Committing to a Journey of Inner Exploration and Growth

Acknowledging personal needs and setting healthy boundaries are essential aspects of cultivating self-love. It is crucial to recognize that your needs are valid and deserve attention. Often, individuals tend to prioritize the needs of others over their own, neglecting their well-being in the process. However, ignoring your own needs can lead to burnout and resentment. By acknowledging and addressing your personal needs, you are taking care of yourself and ensuring that you can show up fully for others in a sustainable way.

Setting healthy boundaries is another key component of self-love. Boundaries guide how you want to be treated and what you are willing to accept in your relationships and interactions. Establishing boundaries is an act of self-respect and self-preservation. It allows you to protect your emotional and mental well-being by clearly communicating your limits and values to others. Remember that it is okay to say no when something doesn't align with your boundaries.

To acknowledge your personal needs effectively, start by tuning into your emotions and physical sensations. Pay attention to how certain situations or interactions make you feel. If something consistently drains your energy or causes negative emotions, it may be a sign that your needs are not being met. Practice self-reflection regularly to identify patterns and triggers that indicate unmet needs.

When setting boundaries, be clear and assertive in communicating your limits. Express your boundaries calmly but firmly, without feeling the need to justify or apologize for them. Consistency is key in maintaining boundaries, so reinforce them through words and actions. Surround yourself with individuals who respect your boundaries and support your well-being.

In the journey toward self-love, remember that prioritizing yourself is not selfish but necessary for your overall health and happiness. By acknowledging your needs and setting healthy boundaries, you create a foundation of self-respect and self-care that supports your well-being. Embrace the power of saying yes to yourself and no to anything that compromises your inner peace. This shift towards honouring yourself paves the way for a more fulfilling and authentic life rooted in self-love.

Understanding Self-Kindness and Well-Being

Prioritizing self-kindness and well-being is not a luxury but a necessity for a fulfilling life. It involves treating oneself with the same compassion and care one would offer to a beloved friend or family member. **Self-kindness** means acknowledging one's mistakes and imperfections without harsh judgment and understanding that being human entails making errors and learning from them. It is about fostering a gentle inner dialogue that uplifts rather than criticizes.

On the other hand, well-being encompasses various aspects of our lives, including physical, emotional, and mental health. It involves recognizing when we need rest, when we need to seek help, or when we need to say no to additional responsibilities. Prioritizing well-being means understanding that taking care of ourselves enables us to better care for others in the long run. It is not selfish; it is an act of self-respect and preservation.

Embracing self-kindness and prioritizing well-being can feel like a radical shift for many who are accustomed to putting others' needs before their own. It requires rewiring ingrained beliefs about self-sacrifice and realizing that self-care is not indulgent but essential for overall wellness. Individuals can build resilience and emotional strength by nurturing a mindset that values kindness towards oneself and prioritizes well-being.

Implementing Self-Kindness Practices

To incorporate self-kindness into daily life, start by observing your inner dialogue. Notice how you speak to yourself in moments of challenge or difficulty. Replace self-criticism with words of encouragement and understanding. Practice self-compassion by treating yourself with the same warmth you would offer a dear friend facing a challenging situation.

Set boundaries that safeguard your well-being without guilt. Learn to say no when you feel overwhelmed or stretched thin. Prioritize activities that bring you joy and relaxation, even if they seem trivial in the grand scheme of responsibilities. Remember that **self-care** is not selfish; it is necessary for maintaining balance and harmony in your life.

Nurturing Well-Being

Well-being encompasses physical health through regular exercise, balanced nutrition, and sufficient rest. Emotional well-being involves processing feelings openly, seeking support when needed, and engaging in activities that bring joy and fulfilment.

Mental well-being includes practicing mindfulness, engaging in hobbies that stimulate your mind, and seeking professional help if struggling with mental health challenges.

By nurturing your overall well-being, you invest in a healthier, more resilient version of yourself. Recognize that self-nurturing is not only beneficial for you but also for those around you who benefit from interacting with a happier, more balanced individual.

Incorporating self-kindness practices and prioritizing well-being may initially feel unfamiliar or uncomfortable for those unaccustomed to focusing on themselves. However, over time, these actions become second nature as you witness their positive impact on your life and relationships. Embrace the journey towards self-love by nurturing yourself with kindness and prioritizing your well-being each day.

Embracing self-love is a transformative journey that starts with a fundamental shift from self-sacrifice to self-nurturing. This chapter has illuminated the crucial distinctions between superficial self-care and cultivating deep, meaningful self-love. By understanding these differences, you are better equipped to embark on a path that truly honours and values your well-being.

Recognizing your own worth is the first step towards self-love.

It requires you to look inward and acknowledge your personal needs without judgment. Setting healthy boundaries is not just a protective measure; it's a profound expression of self-respect. When you assert these boundaries, you communicate to yourself and others that your needs and feelings are valid and important.

Treating oneself with kindness is another cornerstone of self-love. It's about giving yourself permission to prioritize your well-being without feeling guilty. This might mean saying no to additional responsibilities, taking time for rest, or engaging in activities that nourish your soul. Remember, being kind to yourself also means being patient with your progress and compassionate towards your setbacks.

As you move forward, carry with you the understanding that self-love is an active choice that requires consistent effort and dedication. It's about making daily decisions that reflect a commitment to your health and happiness. By doing so, you not only enhance your quality of life but also set a powerful example for those around you.

Start small if you need to, perhaps by dedicating a few minutes each day to meditation or journaling. These moments of introspection can help reinforce your commitment to self-nurturing practices. Over time, these small actions will accumulate, significantly changing how you view and treat yourself.

Remember, the journey to unshakable self-love is profoundly personal and can sometimes be challenging. However, the rewards of such a transformation are immeasurable—not only will you feel more at peace with yourself, but this harmony extends outward, positively affecting all areas of your life.

Embrace this journey with openness and courage, knowing that each step forward is a step towards the love you truly deserve.

Chapter 3: Unveiling the Mask: Confronting Societal Expectations

"The most terrifying thing is to accept oneself completely."
Carl Jung

Are You Wearing the Mask Society Gave You?

In a world that incessantly broadcasts messages about how we should look, act, and feel, it's no wonder many of us grapple with self-doubt. This barrage of societal expectations can be particularly oppressive for women, who often find themselves at the intersection of critiques on appearance, career success, and personal life. The pressure to conform to these ideals undermines self-esteem and obstructs the path to genuine self-acceptance.

The influence of societal norms and beauty standards is profound and far-reaching. Every day, women are bombarded with images and narratives that uphold a narrow standard of beauty and success. These standards are not only unrealistic but are often entirely disconnected from the realities of everyday life. This constant exposure leads many to a relentless cycle of comparison and self-criticism. It's crucial to **analyze** these imposed ideals to understand how they contribute to our feelings of inadequacy.

However, recognizing these pressures is just the beginning. The journey towards self-acceptance demands that we challenge these external voices. It requires redefining our values beyond what society dictates as desirable or acceptable. This means looking inward and affirming qualities that resonate with our deepest selves rather than those applauded by external entities.

Embracing one's true self amidst this noise is no small feat—it's an act of rebellion. Developing strategies to resist external pressures is essential to aid in this rebellion. These practical steps can fortify one's sense of self, whether it's curating media consumption to include more diverse representations of women or engaging in affirmations that center personal strengths over perceived shortcomings.

Empowerment comes from action. We reclaim control over our

self-perception by actively choosing which influences we allow into our lives and how we respond to them. This empowerment is critical for individual well-being and for challenging the broader cultural narratives that shape these pressures.

Support systems play a pivotal role in this transformational process. Surrounding oneself with people who uplift and support one's true self can counteract the often overwhelming tide of societal expectations. These alliances foster an environment where personal worth is affirmed regularly, which is vital for sustained self-acceptance.

Each step taken on this path enhances personal growth and acts as a beacon for others who might be struggling with similar issues. By sharing our stories and strategies, we create a ripple effect that can gradually transform societal norms.

In essence, confronting societal expectations is not just about battling external pressures; it's about internal transformation—turning self-doubt into a resilient, unshakeable form of self-love and acceptance. It's about removing the mask that society hands us and proudly showing the world our true faces. Each small victory in this personal battle contributes to a larger cultural shift towards diversity in beauty, success, and value systems—ultimately leading to a more inclusive world where everyone can thrive without fear of judgment or rejection.

Societal norms and beauty standards often wield a powerful influence, especially on women, shaping perceptions of self-worth and beauty. The relentless bombardment of idealized images in media and the pressure to conform to certain standards can fuel feelings of inadequacy and self-doubt. From airbrushed magazine covers to carefully curated social media feeds, the portrayal of flawless beauty can create an unattainable benchmark many struggle to meet. The constant comparison to these unrealistic standards can lead to a sense of never feeling "enough" as individuals strive to fit into a mold that was never designed to accommodate the diversity of human beauty.

Women are particularly susceptible to the impact of societal expectations, often being judged for their appearance and success in careers and relationships. The subtle yet pervasive messages about how a woman should look, act, and achieve can chip away at self-esteem, fostering a culture of self-criticism and doubt. The pressure to juggle multiple roles while maintaining an impeccable facade can be overwhelming, leaving many women feeling like they are constantly falling short of the mark set by society.

The insidious nature of these expectations lies in their ability to seep into the subconscious, shaping beliefs about one's worth and desirability. Internalizing these standards can lead to negative self-talk, where individuals berate themselves for not meeting an inherently unattainable ideal. The quest for perfection becomes a never-ending battle, magnifying and scrutinizing each perceived flaw or deviation from the norm.

Recognizing the detrimental impact of societal norms is the first step towards reclaiming one's sense of self-worth. By understanding how external influences shape internal narratives, individuals can begin to challenge these ingrained beliefs and redefine beauty on their own terms. Embracing authenticity and self-acceptance becomes a radical act of defiance against a system that thrives on insecurity and comparison.

Unraveling the Layers of Societal Expectations Reveals the Opportunity for True Liberation and Empowerment

In a world filled with societal expectations and rigid beauty standards, it's easy to feel overwhelmed and lost trying to meet these unattainable ideals. As women, the pressure to conform to these norms can be particularly stifling, leading to a constant battle with self-doubt and feelings of inadequacy. However, it's essential to challenge and redefine personal values beyond what society dictates to reclaim your sense of self-worth and identity.

- **Questioning the Status Quo**: One crucial step in this journey is to question the status quo. Ask yourself why certain standards are upheld and who benefits from them. Critically analyzing these norms can unravel their hold over your self-perception. Remember that societal expectations are often constructed and perpetuated by external influences, not intrinsic truths.

- **Identifying Your Authentic Values**: Take the time to reflect on what truly matters to you beyond external validation. What values do you hold dear, regardless of whether they align with societal norms? You can build a stronger foundation for self-acceptance and confidence by identifying and embracing your authentic values.

- **Cultivating Self-Compassion**: Self-compassion is key to challenging societal expectations. Treat yourself with the same kindness and understanding that you would offer a friend facing similar struggles. Acknowledge that it's okay not to fit into a predetermined mold and that your worth is not defined by arbitrary standards set by society.

- **Celebrating Individuality**: Embrace your uniqueness and celebrate what sets you apart from the crowd. Instead of striving for conformity, highlight your strengths, quirks, and talents. Remember that diversity makes the world vibrant and beautiful, and there is immense power in being true to yourself.

- **Setting Boundaries**: Establishing boundaries is crucial in redefining personal values beyond societal norms. Learn to say no to things that do not align with your authentic self or bring you joy. You create space for genuine growth and self-fulfilment by prioritising your well-being and happiness.

- **Seeking Support**: Surround yourself with a supportive community that uplifts and empowers you on your journey of self-discovery. Connect with like-minded individuals who understand the importance of authenticity and self-acceptance. Seeking support can provide encouragement and validation as you navigate away from societal expectations towards a more fulfilling path.

- **Embracing Growth**: Remember that growth is a continuous process. It's okay to stumble along the way or have moments of doubt; what's important is how you pick yourself up and keep moving forward. Embrace challenges as learning and personal development opportunities, knowing that each step away from societal norms brings you closer to genuine self-acceptance.

Challenging societal expectations and redefining personal values based on authenticity and self-love will pave the way for a more fulfilling and empowered existence. Embrace your uniqueness, cultivate self-compassion, set boundaries, seek support, and celebrate your individuality as you embark on this transformative journey toward unshakable self-acceptance.

By implementing these strategies into your daily life, you can resist external pressures and embrace the beauty of being authentically yourself. Remember that self-love is a journey requiring patience, practice, and perseverance. Stay committed to honoring your true self, free from the constraints of societal expectations, and watch as your inner light shines brighter than ever before.

As we navigate the complexities of societal expectations, it's crucial to remember that the journey toward self-acceptance is both necessary and rewarding. The pressures to meet certain standards, especially for women, often lead to a harmful cycle of self-doubt and comparison. However, by analyzing these norms, challenging personal values, and developing resistance strategies, you can dismantle these barriers and foster a healthier self-image.

Recognize the impact of societal norms on your perception of self-worth. These influences are powerful but not definitive.

Acknowledge them as external pressures that do not have to dictate your inner narrative. It's essential to separate your true self from these imposed ideals and understand that worthiness is inherent, not conditional upon meeting specific standards.

Challenging and redefining your values is more than an act of defiance; it's an act of liberation. By identifying what truly matters to you, independent of societal expectations, you carve out a space for genuine self-expression and fulfillment. This step is not about rejecting all norms but discerning which aspects align with your authentic self.

Lastly, developing strategies to resist external pressures is critical. Simple actions like curating your media consumption, engaging in affirmative practices like positive self-talk, and surrounding yourself with supportive relationships can shield you from negative influences. These practices empower you to embrace your true identity, fostering resilience against the tide of societal expectations.

Remember, every step to understand and resist these norms is a step toward embracing the love you deserve. This journey is about reclaiming your narrative and affirming that you are enough as you are. Let each strategy be a building block in constructing a life defined not by how well you conform but by how authentically you live.

Embrace this transformative journey with courage and conviction. The path to unshakable self-love isn't without its challenges, but it's rich with rewards that resonate deeply within the fabric of who you are. Stand firm in your truth, and let your actions reflect your innate worth.

Chapter 4: Rejecting Selfishness Myths: Embracing Self-Love for Healthy Relationships

"Until you value yourself, you won't value your time. Until you value your time, you will not do anything with it."

M. Scott Peck

Is Loving Yourself Really Selfish?

The notion that self-love equates to selfishness is widespread and deeply ingrained in many cultures and societies. Yet, this belief is fundamentally flawed. **Self-love is essential**, not just for individual well-being, but also for the health and authenticity of our relationships with others. This chapter delves into the myths surrounding self-love, illustrating why it's crucial and how it serves as a cornerstone for nurturing healthier, more genuine

56

connections.

Many people have a misconception that focusing on oneself is an act of negligence towards others. This couldn't be further from the truth. By embracing self-love, we equip ourselves with the emotional resilience and strength necessary to engage more fully and compassionately in our relationships. It's about filling your cup so abundantly that it overflows to nourish those around you. Recognizing this can transform how we interact with the world.

Debunking the myths surrounding self-love is our starting point. The belief that caring for oneself is inherently selfish often leads to burnout and resentment—neither healthy nor conducive to fostering positive relationships. Challenging these misconceptions opens us to a life where self-care and caring for others coexist harmoniously.

Furthermore, self-love enables authenticity in our interactions with others. When you are true to yourself, you establish honesty in your relationships. This authenticity attracts like-minded individuals and deepens relationships as genuine interactions replace superficial exchanges.

But how do we balance self-care with caring for others? It begins by recognizing that self-care isn't a zero-sum game. Caring for oneself actually enriches our capacity to care for others effectively. Practical strategies include setting clear boundaries, prioritizing time for self-reflection, and engaging in activities that replenish rather than drain your energy.

Taking control of your emotional well-being by actively engaging in self-love practices is beneficial and necessary. It allows you to navigate life's challenges with greater ease and confidence, fostering an environment where you and your relationships can thrive.

As we explore these concepts further, remember: your journey towards self-love isn't just about improving your own life—it's about enriching the lives of those around you, too. Through actionable advice and compassionate understanding, this chapter aims to guide you toward more profound self-acceptance and more fulfilling relationships. Embracing self-love is not only an act of self-respect but an act of generosity towards those you love.

Self-love is often misunderstood, with many believing it to be a selfish act. The misconception that prioritizing oneself equates to neglecting others can hinder individuals from embracing self-love fully. However, the truth is quite the opposite. By nurturing self-love, individuals can show up more authentically and compassionately in their relationships. When we care for ourselves, we are better equipped to care for others effectively and lead more balanced, content lives.

Contrary to popular belief, self-love is not about self-centeredness but self-respect and self-compassion. Caring for oneself is a fundamental aspect of being able to care for others. When we neglect our well-being, we deplete our internal resources, making it challenging to be there for others meaningfully. Self-love is not a zero-sum game; it is about creating a harmonious balance between caring for oneself and caring for others.

The idea that self-love is selfish often stems from societal norms prioritizing external validation over internal fulfilment. This misconception can lead individuals to put their needs last, leading to burnout and resentment in relationships. Embracing self-love means recognizing that taking care of ourselves benefits our well-being and enhances our ability to support and uplift those around us.

Rejecting the myth that self-love is selfish requires a shift in perspective. It involves understanding that prioritizing oneself is not an act of egoism but an act of self-preservation. When we love ourselves, we set a positive example for how we deserve to be treated by others. By debunking the myth that self-love is selfish, individuals can pave the way for healthier relationships built on mutual respect and care.

The Role of Self-Love in Building Authentic Relationships

Self-love is not a solitary journey; it is the cornerstone that enables us to show up authentically in our relationships with others. When prioritizing self-love, we are better equipped to offer genuine compassion and empathy to those around us. By nurturing a healthy relationship with ourselves, we create a solid foundation for building meaningful connections with others. It is not selfish to put ourselves first; it is essential for fostering healthy and fulfilling relationships with those we care about.

Authenticity is key in relationships and stems from a place of self-assurance and self-acceptance. When we love ourselves unconditionally, we are likelier to be honest and open with others, leading to deeper and more meaningful connections.

Self-love allows us to set boundaries that protect our well-being while also respecting the boundaries of those around us. It empowers us to communicate our needs effectively and listen empathetically to the needs of others.

Self-love fosters empathy as we become more attuned to our

own emotions and experiences, making us more understanding of the feelings and experiences of others. When we care for ourselves, we are better equipped to care for those around us, offering support and compassion from a place of strength rather than depletion. It is not selfish to prioritize self-care; it is an act of kindness towards ourselves that ultimately benefits everyone.

Healthy relationships thrive on mutual respect, understanding, and support. When we practice self-love, we model healthy behaviours for those around us, inspiring them to do the same.

Self-love sets a positive example of how relationships should be nurtured with kindness, compassion, and authenticity. By valuing ourselves, we teach others how to value us as well.

Self-love is the key to cultivating harmonious relationships built on trust, respect, and genuine connection. By embracing self-love, we create space for vulnerability and authenticity in our interactions with others. Through loving ourselves, we can truly love others, creating a ripple effect of positivity and compassion in our relationships and beyond.

Self-care is not a selfish act; it is a fundamental practice that allows individuals to show up fully in their relationships. Balancing self-care with caring for others is essential for maintaining healthy connections and overall well-being.

Prioritizing self-care does not mean neglecting the needs of those around you but rather ensuring that you can offer genuine support and compassion. You are better equipped to care for others effectively when you care for yourself.

Setting boundaries is a crucial aspect of balancing self-care with caring for others. It involves recognizing your limits and communicating them clearly to those around you. Establishing boundaries protects your energy and prevents burnout, allowing you to show up more authentically in your relationships. Boundaries are not walls; they are bridges that promote healthier connections by fostering respect and understanding between individuals.

Practice self-compassion as you navigate the delicate balance between self-care and caring for others. Be kind to yourself when you feel overwhelmed or guilty for prioritizing your needs. Self-compassion cultivates resilience and emotional strength, enabling you to approach challenges gracefully and with understanding. Remember that it is okay to put yourself first sometimes; you cannot pour from an empty cup.

Allocate time for self-care without guilt. Schedule moments in your day dedicated solely to activities that nourish your mind, body, and soul. Whether reading a book, walking, or practicing mindfulness, make self-care a non-negotiable part of your routine. Investing in yourself is not selfish; it is an act of self-love that benefits everyone around you.

Engage in open communication with your loved ones about your needs and boundaries. Expressing your feelings and desires openly fosters deeper connections based on mutual respect and understanding. Healthy relationships thrive on honest and transparent communication, allowing both parties to support each other authentically.

Seek support when needed. Recognizing when you require assistance or guidance to balance self-care and caring for others is essential. Whether through therapy, support groups, or trusted friends, reaching out for help is a sign of strength, not weakness. You do not have to navigate this journey alone.

As we've explored throughout this chapter, the belief that self-love equates to selfishness is a profound misconception. Embracing self-love is not about neglecting others but about fostering personal well-being that enriches our interactions and relationships. When you prioritize your emotional and mental health, you are better equipped to support and connect with those around you.

Understanding and implementing self-love allows us to approach relationships with a sense of completeness rather than seeking validation or fulfilment from others. This shift alleviates pressure from our relationships and leads to more genuine and supportive connections. Remember, caring deeply for oneself is the first step in offering genuine care to others. By balancing self-care with the care of those around us, we create a harmonious give-and-take that benefits everyone involved.

To integrate these insights into your daily life, start with small, manageable steps toward self-care. Whether setting aside time for meditation, pursuing a hobby you love, or simply saying no when you're overstretched, each act of self-love is a building block towards a healthier, more fulfilling life. Your ability to love yourself directly influences how you love others, making self-love a crucial component of healthy relationships.

Let's understand that self-love propels us towards more authentic and compassionate living. It encourages us to show up as our best selves for the people we care about and for our communities. By rejecting the myths surrounding self-love, we open ourselves to a life characterized by deeper fulfilment and more resilient relationships.

Embrace this journey with confidence, knowing that the path to improved relationships and personal contentment lies in recognizing the value of your own well-being. As you continue practicing self-love, watch your world transform, enriched by healthier relationships and unwavering self-respect.

Chapter 5: Committing to the Journey: The Active Pursuit of Self-Love

"Self-love is the source of all our other loves."

Pierre Corneille

Are You Truly Loving Yourself or Just Going Through the Motions?

Self-love is often misunderstood as a static state of being—something to achieve and check off a list. However, true self-love is dynamic, evolving alongside us as we journey through life. It's not merely about feeling good about ourselves in isolated moments of success. Still, it involves a deep, consistent practice of nurturing our well-being and happiness in the face of life's inevitable challenges. This requires intention, commitment, and perseverance—a far cry from passive self-acceptance.

The path to genuine self-love is fraught with obstacles, primarily our own internalized patterns of self-criticism and limiting beliefs. These barriers can make the journey seem daunting. Yet, it is precise that the pursuit of self-love becomes truly rewarding because these challenges are tough. Understanding self-love as an active practice necessitates recognizing its necessity and committing to it as a regular part of our lives.

We must first identify and confront our old negative self-talk and self-criticism patterns to embark on this transformative journey. These are often deeply ingrained and automatic, making them difficult to detect without conscious effort. However, recognizing these patterns is essential for setting the stage for their replacement with thoughts grounded in self-compassion and acceptance.

Replacing negative thought patterns with positive affirmations and gratitude practices isn't just about feeling better now—it's about rewiring our brains to default to compassion rather than criticism. This shift doesn't happen overnight; it requires daily practice and dedication, like muscle training. Each day presents a new opportunity to reinforce this mindset, building resilience against old habits of self-doubt.

Moreover, developing a personal action plan tailored to individual needs and lifestyles is crucial for sustaining this practice. This plan should include specific, daily actions that foster self-love—from mindfulness exercises like meditation to physical activities that honor one's body and emotional health. Additionally, setting realistic goals within this plan helps maintain focus and motivation throughout this process.

Step-by-Step Guide: Cultivating Self-Love Daily

Reflect on Old Patterns

Take time each day to reflect on instances where critical thoughts emerged. Recognize patterns or triggers that may cause these thoughts to surface.

Challenge and Replace Negative Thoughts

Actively challenge these criticisms by questioning their validity and replace them with affirmations that promote acceptance and love towards oneself.

Daily Affirmations

Create a set of personal affirmations that resonate with your desires for self-worth and peace. Repeat them morning and night, making them a cornerstone of your daily routine.

Gratitude Journaling

Each evening, write down three aspects of your day or yourself that you are grateful for. This shifts focus from what's lacking to appreciating what is abundant in your life.

Self-Compassion Meditation

Incorporate at least five minutes of meditation focusing on breathing kindness towards oneself and accepting one's imperfections as part of being human.

Visualization Exercises

Regularly visualize achieving your goals related to self-love; see yourself living as a person who loves themselves unconditionally.

Celebrate Small Victories

Acknowledge every small success along your journey. Whether it's sticking to your daily affirmations or handling a stressful situation with grace, celebrate it.

Surround Yourself with Positivity

Ensure your environment reflects the positivity you wish to cultivate within yourself—limit interactions with toxic influences where possible.

Practice Self-Care

Dedicate weekly time to engage in activities that rejuvenate both body and soul through yoga, reading, or spending time in nature.

Seek Professional Support

If obstacles feel insurmountable, consider seeking counselling or therapy focused on building self-esteem and managing negative thought patterns.

This systematic approach provides structure and adapts over time as you evolve. It acknowledges that setbacks are part of the process while celebrating growth. By committing to this daily practice, you transform fleeting moments of self-appreciation into a continuous journey of deepening self-love—where every step forward enriches the profound relationship you cultivate with yourself.

Self-love is not a destination to reach but a journey to commit to. It requires ongoing effort, intention, and perseverance. Cultivating self-love is an active practice that demands dedication to unlearning old patterns of self-criticism and embracing self-compassion. It involves making a conscious daily choice to prioritize self-care, set boundaries, and challenge limiting beliefs that hinder our growth. Self-love is not a passive state that will magically appear; it is an active pursuit that we must engage with consistently.

In this self-love journey, it's essential to understand that setbacks and challenges are inevitable. There will be days when self-doubt creeps in or when old insecurities resurface. However, it's crucial to remember that these moments do not define our progress. Self-love is about the commitment to keep going despite obstacles and showing compassion even in struggle. It's a journey marked by resilience and the willingness to try again, even when difficult.

One of the key aspects of actively pursuing self-love is the willingness to confront our inner critic. Identifying old patterns of self-criticism is a crucial step in transforming them into self-compassion. This process involves recognizing when we are being harsh or judgmental towards ourselves and consciously responding with kindness and understanding instead. By challenging our negative self-talk and replacing it with affirming words, we can gradually shift our mindset towards self-acceptance.

Self-love also requires us to develop daily habits and mindset shifts that support our well-being. This may include journaling, meditation, exercise, or engaging in activities that bring us joy. Incorporating these habits into our routine reinforces the message that we are worthy of care and attention. Consistency in these practices is key to nurturing self-love and making it a natural part of our daily lives.

Embracing Self-Love as an Active Journey Means Committing to Ourselves Wholeheartedly, Even on the Toughest Days

Identifying and replacing old patterns of self-criticism with self-compassion is a crucial step in the journey toward self-love. Many have internalized negative beliefs about themselves, often stemming from past experiences, societal standards, or comparisons with others. These patterns of self-criticism can be deeply ingrained, shaping how we view ourselves and interact with the world. Recognizing these destructive thought patterns is the first step towards breaking free from their grip.

One effective strategy to combat self-criticism is practicing self-compassion. Instead of harshly judging ourselves for perceived flaws or mistakes, we can cultivate a kinder inner dialogue acknowledging our humanity and imperfections. Self-compassion involves treating oneself with the same warmth and understanding that we would offer to a close friend facing a challenge. This shift in perspective can help break the cycle of negative self-talk and foster a sense of acceptance and kindness towards oneself.

Another powerful tool in replacing self-criticism with self-compassion is practicing gratitude. Focusing on what we appreciate about ourselves and our lives can counteract feelings of unworthiness or inadequacy that often fuel self-criticism. Regularly reflecting on our strengths, accomplishments, and the positive aspects of our lives can help cultivate a sense of self-worth and appreciation for who we are.

Setting boundaries is also essential in overcoming patterns of self-criticism. Learning to say no to unrealistic demands or toxic relationships and prioritizing our needs and well-being is an act of self-love that reinforces our worthiness. Establishing boundaries that honor our values and protect our emotional health creates space for self-compassion to flourish.

Practicing mindfulness can further aid in replacing self-criticism with self-compassion. By staying present in the moment and observing our thoughts without judgment, we can cultivate a greater awareness of our inner critic and choose to respond with kindness instead. Mindfulness practices such as meditation or deep breathing exercises can help quiet the voice of self-criticism and create room for self-compassion to thrive.

Self-Love Action Plan Framework: The Path to Personal Transformation

The Self-Love Action Plan Framework is designed to guide you through developing a personalized strategy for embracing self-love, enhancing self-care practices, and fostering a mindset shift towards self-compassion. By following this framework, you will embark on a journey of self-discovery and empowerment, taking concrete steps to prioritize your well-being and nurture a loving relationship with yourself.

Self-Assessment: Understanding Your Starting Point

The first step in creating your action plan is to conduct a thorough **self-assessment**. This involves reflecting on your current self-love and self-care practices, identifying areas where you excel, and recognizing areas that require improvement. By clarifying your strengths and weaknesses in this area, you can effectively tailor your action plan to address specific needs.

S.M.A.R.T Goal Setting: Clear and Achievable Objectives

Once you have assessed your starting point, the next step is establishing **S.M.A.R.T. goals** for your self-love journey. These goals should be Specific, Measurable, Attainable, Relevant, and Time-Bound. For example, setting a goal to practice daily affirmations or allocating time for self-reflection are tangible objectives that contribute to nurturing self-love effectively.

Holistic Approach: Balancing Physical, Emotional, Mental, and Spiritual Well-Being

Your action plan should encompass all dimensions of well-being to ensure a holistic approach to self-love. This includes focusing on physical activities that promote health, engaging in emotional practices that nurture resilience and positivity, adopting mental exercises that enhance self-awareness and mindfulness, and incorporating spiritual rituals that align with your beliefs and values.

Integration into Daily Routine: Making Self-Love a Priority

Integrating self-love practices into your daily routine is crucial to make your action plan sustainable and effective. Consider your unique life circumstances and time constraints when scheduling these activities. Whether dedicating time in the morning for meditation or setting boundaries during work hours to prioritize self-care, find ways to weave these practices seamlessly into your day.

Flexibility and Adaptability: Adjusting Along the Way

Recognize that self-love is an ongoing journey that may require adjustments. Stay open to flexibility in your action plan by regularly reviewing and refining your goals and practices. This adaptability ensures your plan remains relevant and aligned with your evolving needs and aspirations.

Overcoming Barriers: Strategies for Success

As you implement your action plan, you may encounter common barriers such as guilt over prioritizing yourself or challenges forming new habits. Practical tips can help you overcome these obstacles. For instance, reframing guilt as an essential part of self-care or using visual cues to reinforce new habits can support your journey toward self-love.

Celebrating Progress: Acknowledging Your Growth

Lastly, remember to celebrate even the smallest victories along the way. Celebrating progress reinforces positive behaviours and motivates continued efforts toward cultivating self-love. Whether journaling about achievements or treating yourself kindly when setbacks occur, acknowledging your growth is essential in nurturing a compassionate relationship with yourself.

Following this Self-Love Action Plan Framework empowers you to embark on a transformative journey towards embracing self-love as a fundamental aspect of your well-being. You pave the way for personal transformation and lasting self-acceptance through intentional practice and commitment to nurturing yourself with kindness and compassion.

Embracing the journey of self-love is more than a momentary affirmation; it's a **daily commitment** to nurturing your well-being and happiness. This chapter has taught you that self-love is an active, ongoing practice that requires perseverance and dedication. By identifying old patterns of self-criticism and replacing them with self-compassion, you are setting the foundation for a transformative life experience.

Every step you take towards recognizing your worth and embracing kindness towards yourself is a step towards a more fulfilled life. The personal self-love action plan you've developed is not just a tool but a roadmap to consistently apply these practices in your daily life. Remember, the small habits you incorporate today can lead to profound changes over time.

It's important to acknowledge that the path to self-love might sometimes be challenging. You may encounter setbacks or old habits creeping back in. However, armed with the strategies outlined, you have the power to navigate these challenges effectively. Consistent practice is beneficial and crucial for making self-love a sustainable part of who you are.

Let this chapter remind you that your journey to self-love is uniquely yours. It's perfectly okay to move at your own pace and tailor the strategies to fit your needs and circumstances. You possess all the tools required to overcome any hurdles along the way.

As you continue this journey, remember that every effort you make is building towards a greater sense of peace and acceptance within yourself. Engage actively with your self-love plan, adjust it as needed, and celebrate every small victory. Your commitment to this process reflects your strength and determination to live a life filled with the love you deserve.

Embrace this journey wholeheartedly, knowing each step forward shapes a more compassionate relationship with yourself. Here's to moving forward with confidence, resilience, and an unwavering commitment to growth and happiness.

Chapter 6: Building Your Self-Love Toolkit: Compassion, Acceptance, and Presence

"Loving yourself isn't vanity. It's sanity."

Katrina Mayer

Unveil the Power of Self-Compassion in Your Life

Self-love is more than a feel-good term; it's a robust framework for emotional resilience and self-acceptance. At the heart of this transformative journey are the principles of self-compassion and self-acceptance. These aren't just buzzwords—they are practical tools that can dramatically shift how you relate to yourself, especially when navigating the challenges of a busy life.

Self-compassion involves treating yourself with the kindness and understanding you would offer a good friend. It's about recognizing that imperfection is part of the human condition and responding to personal failings with kindness rather than judgment. This chapter will explore how integrating self-compassion into your daily routine can fortify your mental and emotional well-being.

On the other hand, self-acceptance is about embracing all aspects of yourself—your strengths and flaws. It's an acknowledgment of your worthiness, regardless of your achievements or setbacks. This chapter will guide you through practical steps to cultivate a deeper acceptance of yourself, which is crucial for building authentic self-love.

Embrace the Present: Mindfulness as a Tool for Self-Acceptance

Mindfulness and meditation are not just practices for spiritual enthusiasts—they are accessible tools that can help anyone enhance their self-awareness and live more fully in the present moment. By incorporating mindfulness into your life, you learn to observe your thoughts and feelings without judgment. This practice fosters a profound sense of peace and acceptance, essential for nurturing self-love.

Meditation, in particular, offers a structured way to practice mindfulness. It allows you to set aside dedicated time to focus on being present. This chapter provides simple meditation techniques that can be woven into even the busiest schedules, ensuring everyone can benefit from this powerful practice.

Cultivating Compassionate Inner Dialogue: Transform How You Talk to Yourself

The language we use with ourselves influences our self-perception and overall mental health. A critical inner voice can increase stress and diminished self-esteem, while a compassionate inner dialogue builds resilience and confidence. This chapter will offer strategies to transform your inner speech patterns into more supportive and empowering conversations.

Practicing positive affirmations, setting realistic expectations, and acknowledging your achievements are ways to enhance your internal dialogue. By changing how you talk to yourself, you actively reinforce self-love, improving every aspect of your life.

Daily Practices That Anchor Self-Love

Consistency is key when building any skill, especially one that is as fundamental as self-love. This chapter outlines daily practices that embed compassion, acceptance, and mindfulness into your routine. These activities are designed to be manageable and impactful, whether through journaling, reflective exercises, or structured meditative practices.

Each practice is crafted with busy schedules in mind, ensuring that even on your busiest days, you have accessible tools to maintain emotional balance and foster ongoing self-acceptance.

By embracing these principles and practices, you empower yourself to lead a more contented, peaceful life. You learn that self-love isn't just about feeling good—it's about cultivating a compassionate relationship with yourself that stands the test of time and challenge. As you implement these tools, remember that every step is closer to the profound acceptance and love you deserve.

Self-compassion and self-acceptance are foundational pillars of building a strong sense of self-love. **Self-compassion** involves treating oneself with kindness and understanding, as one would offer a close friend in times of suffering or failure. It is about acknowledging that imperfection is part of the human experience and responding to oneself with empathy rather than self-criticism. **On the other hand, self-acceptance** entails recognizing and embracing all aspects of oneself, including strengths, weaknesses, successes, and failures, without judgment or conditions.

Integrating self-compassion and self-acceptance into daily life requires a shift in mindset. Instead of being overly critical or demanding perfection from oneself, it involves cultivating a gentler and more forgiving inner dialogue. By practicing self-compassion, individuals can navigate challenges with resilience and self-kindness, fostering a sense of worthiness and belonging within themselves.

One key aspect of integrating self-compassion and self-acceptance is acknowledging the inner critic. The inner critic is that voice inside our heads that often magnifies our flaws, doubts our abilities, and highlights our shortcomings. By becoming aware of this critical voice and challenging its validity, individuals can begin reframing their thoughts more compassionately and accepting.

Self-care practices play a crucial role in nurturing self-compassion and self-acceptance. Engaging in activities that promote relaxation, creativity, or connection with others can help individuals cultivate a sense of well-being and worthiness. This can include anything from taking a warm bath to journaling about one's emotions or spending quality time with loved ones.

Incorporating self-affirmations into daily routines can also reinforce feelings of self-compassion and acceptance. By regularly repeating positive statements about oneself, individuals can challenge negative beliefs and build a more positive self-image.

Developing a support system that includes friends, family members, or even support groups can provide additional validation and encouragement on the journey toward self-love. Surrounding oneself with people who uplift and affirm one's worth can reinforce feelings of acceptance and compassion.

Nurturing Self-Love Through Mindfulness and Meditation

Practicing mindfulness and meditation is a powerful tool for enhancing self-awareness and acceptance. Individuals can cultivate a deeper understanding of their thoughts, emotions, and behaviours by engaging in these practices, leading to a more profound connection with themselves. Mindfulness involves being fully present in the moment, without judgment or attachment to thoughts or feelings. It allows individuals to observe their inner experiences without getting caught up in them, fostering a sense of clarity and peace.

Meditation, on the other hand, offers a structured approach to train the mind and cultivate awareness. Through regular meditation practice, individuals can develop the ability to focus their attention, quiet the mind, and explore their inner landscape with curiosity and compassion. This process can be particularly beneficial in recognizing self-criticism or negative self-talk patterns, allowing individuals to respond to these thoughts with kindness and understanding.

Self-awareness is key to fostering self-acceptance. By becoming more attuned to their thoughts and emotions through mindfulness and meditation, individuals can identify areas where they may be overly critical or judgmental towards themselves. This increased awareness allows one to challenge negative beliefs and replace them with more compassionate and empowering perspectives.

Through mindfulness practices such as deep breathing exercises, body scans, or guided meditations, individuals can anchor themselves in the present moment and cultivate a sense of peace and acceptance. These practices help individuals develop a non-reactive stance towards their internal experiences, allowing them to respond to challenges with greater resilience and emotional balance.

Incorporating mindfulness and meditation into daily routines can have a transformative impact on one's relationship with oneself. By dedicating even just a few minutes each day to these practices, individuals can nurture a sense of inner calm, clarity, and self-compassion that radiates into all aspects of their lives.

Regular practice is essential for reaping the full benefits of mindfulness and meditation. Consistency is key in developing these skills over time and integrating them into one's daily life. By setting aside dedicated time for reflection and introspection, individuals can deepen their connection with themselves and cultivate a profound sense of self-love and acceptance.

In essence, mindfulness and meditation are powerful tools that enable individuals to cultivate self-awareness, foster self-acceptance, and enhance their overall well-being. By incorporating these practices into their daily routines, individuals can embark on a journey of self-discovery and transformation that leads to a more profound sense of self-love and inner peace.

Cultivate a Compassionate Inner Dialogue

To foster self-love, it is crucial to cultivate a compassionate inner dialogue through daily self-love practices. This internal conversation shapes our self-perception and influences how we approach challenges and setbacks. By implementing simple yet powerful strategies, individuals can transform their self-talk from critical to supportive, nurturing a kinder relationship with themselves.

Practice Positive Affirmations

Start your day by affirming your worth and capabilities. Repeat positive statements about yourself, such as "I am enough," "I am worthy of love," or "I trust in my abilities." These affirmations can counteract negative self-talk and reinforce a more positive self-image.

Express Gratitude

Take a moment each day to reflect on what you are grateful for. Express gratitude for the small joys in life, your accomplishments, or the support you receive from others. Gratitude shifts your focus from what is lacking to what is abundant in your life, fostering a sense of contentment and positivity.

Practice Self-Compassion

When facing challenges or setbacks, extend yourself compassion as you would to a dear friend. Acknowledge your emotions without judgment and offer yourself words of comfort and understanding. Self-compassion builds resilience and self-soothing skills, helping you navigate difficulties more easily.

Challenge Negative Thoughts

Become aware of negative thought patterns and challenge them with evidence-based reasoning. Ask yourself if these thoughts are based on facts or assumptions. By questioning negative beliefs, you can reframe them in a more realistic and compassionate light.

Set Boundaries

Establish clear boundaries that honor your needs and well-being. *Say no when necessary*, prioritize self-care, and communicate your limits to others. Setting boundaries reinforces self-respect and teaches others how to treat you with kindness and consideration.

Practice Self-Care Rituals

Engage in regular self-care rituals that nurture your mind, body, and soul. Set aside time for activities that bring you joy, whether reading a book, relaxing, walking in nature, or practicing yoga. Self-care rituals replenish your energy reserves and cultivate a sense of inner peace.

Reflect on Your Growth

Take time to reflect on your personal growth journey. Celebrate your achievements, no matter how small they may seem. Recognize your progress towards cultivating self-love and acknowledge the resilience and courage it takes to prioritize your well-being.

Integrating these daily practices into your routine allows you to gradually shift towards a more compassionate inner dialogue that fosters genuine self-love. Remember that building self-love is a continuous process that requires patience, persistence, and self-compassion. Embrace each step of this transformative journey with kindness towards yourself.

Building a foundation of self-love is an empowering journey that begins with embracing self-compassion and self-acceptance.

These principles are not just ideas but practical tools that can transform how you view and treat yourself when integrated into your daily life. Self-compassion involves treating yourself with the same kindness and understanding that you would offer to a friend in distress. It's about recognizing that imperfection is part of the human experience and responding to your errors with empathy rather than harsh judgment.

Similarly, self-acceptance is crucial. It allows you to acknowledge your strengths and weaknesses without undue criticism. This acceptance doesn't mean resignation but rather an understanding that you are a work in progress, deserving of love at every stage of your journey. Embracing these aspects of self-love prepares you to handle life's challenges with greater resilience and less self-doubt.

Mindfulness and meditation are powerful practices that support this process. They help you cultivate presence, meaning you live more fully in the current moment rather than being lost in regrets of the past or worries about the future. By enhancing your self-awareness, these practices enable you to recognize negative thought patterns and gently guide them towards more constructive pathways.

Daily self-love practices are essential for nurturing this compassionate inner dialogue. Simple actions like journaling, affirmations, or setting aside time for personal reflection can significantly impact how you relate to yourself over time. These practices ensure that self-love is not just a concept but a lived reality.

Remember, the path to unshakable self-love requires patience and persistence. Each step toward compassion, acceptance, and presence is a step toward a more fulfilling life. You have the innate strength to foster this transformative relationship with yourself. Start small, remain consistent, and watch as the quality of your internal world flourishes alongside your ability to love and accept yourself just as you are.

Embrace these tools; let them guide you to the love you deserve—a love profound, peaceful, and permanently within your reach.

Chapter 7: Daily Practices for a Loving Mindset: Affirmations, Journaling, and Mindfulness

"The first step toward being loved is learning to love what you see when you look in the mirror."

Tadahiko Nagao

Unleash the Power of Self-Love: Daily Tools for Transformation

The journey to self-acceptance is often paved with the challenges of overcoming self-doubt. It's a path that demands persistence, patience, and practical tools designed to reshape our inner dialogue. This essential chapter delves into daily practices that nurture self-love and fundamentally rewire our cognitive processes. Through affirmations, journaling, and mindfulness, we can steadily transform negative thinking patterns into a foundation of strong self-esteem and deep-seated compassion toward ourselves.

Our minds are potent entities capable of both creating and limiting our realities. The persistent echo of negative thoughts can lead to a diminished view of one's worth. However, we initiate a crucial shift towards positivity and empowerment by adopting daily affirmations and engaging in positive self-talk. This practice is about more than just repeating kind words; it's about believing them and allowing them to permeate our consciousness, fostering an environment where self-acceptance thrives.

Journaling stands as a reflective tool that provides clarity and connection. By simply writing down our thoughts, we tap into deeper emotional undercurrents and uncover hidden facets of our psyche. This process isn't just about venting emotions, understanding them, and recognizing patterns that may hold us back. Through guided prompts or free writing, journaling becomes a journey of self-discovery, offering insights vital for personal growth and increased self-awareness.

Mindfulness exercises anchor us in the present moment, where judgment is suspended, and acceptance is cultivated. Practicing mindfulness regularly, whether through breathing exercises or mindful walking, teaches us to observe our experiences without criticism. This fosters an attitude of kindness towards ourselves, smoothing the path towards accepting our imperfections and appreciating our strengths.

Step-by-Step Guide: Crafting Your Compassionate Self

Step 1: Implement Morning Affirmations

Kickstart your day with empowering affirmations. Select phrases that resonate deeply with your aspirations, such as "I am worthy of love and joy" or "I embrace my strength each day." Speak them aloud in front of a mirror to reinforce their power.

Step 2: Journaling for Self-Discovery

Dedicate time each day to write in your journal. Whether responding to specific prompts that challenge you to reflect on recent experiences or expressing whatever comes to mind, this practice helps deepen your relationship with yourself.

Step 3: Mindfulness Exercises

Incorporate simple mindfulness practices into your daily routine. This could be a brief session focusing on your breath or performing a full body scan meditation. These methods help you stay present and reduce stress.

Step 4: Practice Self-Compassion

Remind yourself throughout the day that everyone has challenges and setbacks. Offer yourself the same kindness you would give a friend in distress.

Step 5: Engage in Mindful Eating

Take the time to enjoy each meal without distractions. Notice the textures, flavours, and sensations as you eat, which promotes better digestion and a more satisfying eating experience.

Step 6: Engage Your Senses

Regularly pause to fully experience your surroundings using all your senses. This practice helps draw attention away from negative thoughts and back to the present moment.

Step 7: Practice Gratitude

Reflect on what you're grateful for each day. This could be done by writing down three things you appreciate every night or discussing them over dinner with family.

Step 8: Perform Random Acts of Kindness

Simple acts of kindness towards yourself or others can significantly boost your mood and sense of self-worth.

Step 9: Set Boundaries

Learn to say no to situations that drain your energy and yes to those that enrich it.

Step 10: Reflect and Adjust

Evaluate which practices benefit you the most and make adjustments as necessary. Stay flexible in your approach—what works well one month might need tweaking the next.

By integrating these steps into your daily life, you actively contribute to a more loving mindset towards yourself. Each action taken is a step forward in transforming self-doubt into enduring self-acceptance, leading you closer to the profound love you deserve.

Implementing daily affirmations and positive self-talk is a powerful way to rewire negative thinking patterns and cultivate a more loving mindset toward oneself. Affirmations are simple yet impactful statements that can help shift your perspective from self-criticism to self-compassion. By repeating positive affirmations regularly, you can challenge the negative beliefs you hold about yourself and replace them with more empowering thoughts.

Positive self-talk is another essential practice that involves consciously choosing to speak to yourself kindly and be supportive. Instead of allowing your inner critic to dominate your thoughts, make a conscious effort to speak to yourself as you would to a friend—with kindness, understanding, and encouragement. Changing how you talk to yourself can gradually build a more positive self-image and increase self-esteem.

Daily affirmations and positive self-talk are not about ignoring your challenges or pretending everything is perfect. It's about acknowledging your struggles while recognizing your strengths and potential for growth. These practices help you develop resilience and self-compassion, enabling you to navigate life's ups and downs with a more loving attitude towards yourself.

When incorporating affirmations and positive self-talk into your daily routine, choosing phrases that resonate with you personally is essential. Tailor your affirmations to address areas where you struggle with self-doubt or insecurity. Whether it's about your appearance, abilities, relationships, or worthiness, create affirmations that directly counteract the negative beliefs you hold in those areas.

Consistency is key when it comes to implementing daily affirmations and positive self-talk. Set aside time each day—in the morning, before bed, or throughout the day—to **repeat your affirmations** and practice positive self-talk. The more consistently you engage in these practices, the more they will become ingrained in your thought patterns, leading to a lasting shift towards a more loving mindset.

Be patient with yourself as you incorporate daily affirmations and positive self-talk into your routine. Changing ingrained thought patterns takes time, so be gentle and compassionate as you work on rewiring your mindset. Celebrate small victories along the way and remind yourself that every positive affirmation and kind word you speak to yourself is a step towards nurturing greater self-love.

Deepening Self-Connection Through Journaling and Mindfulness

Journaling can be a powerful tool for self-discovery and fostering a deeper connection with oneself. By engaging in reflective writing, individuals can uncover hidden thoughts, emotions, and beliefs that may influence their self-perception. Journaling prompts serve as guiding questions that prompt introspection and encourage individuals to explore their inner world with honesty and vulnerability. These prompts spark self-awareness, promote healing, and nurture personal growth.

One effective journaling prompt to kickstart self-discovery is to reflect on moments of genuine happiness. Recalling instances when you felt truly content and joyful can help identify activities, people, or environments that resonate with your authentic self. This exercise allows you to pinpoint sources of genuine happiness and align your life more closely with what brings you joy.

Another valuable journaling prompt is to explore limiting beliefs. Uncovering deep-seated beliefs that hold you back from embracing self-love is essential for personal growth. By identifying these negative beliefs, you can challenge them, reframe your mindset, and cultivate a more compassionate view of yourself. Acknowledging these limiting beliefs is the first step towards dismantling them and creating space for self-acceptance.

Gratitude journaling is a simple yet powerful practice that can shift your focus from what is lacking in your life to what you appreciate. Taking time each day to write down things you are grateful for cultivates a mindset of abundance and positivity. This practice helps rewire your brain to notice the good in your life, fostering a sense of gratitude and contentment.

Self-compassion journaling involves writing messages of kindness and understanding to yourself. By treating yourself with the same compassion you would offer a friend in need, you can build a more nurturing relationship with yourself. Acknowledging your struggles, mistakes, and insecurities with compassion allows for healing and growth, fostering a deeper sense of self-love.

Writing letters to your past or future self is a valuable journaling prompt for fostering a connection with oneself. Reflecting on past experiences or envisioning future goals through letter writing can provide clarity, closure, and direction. This exercise allows you to communicate with different versions of yourself, offering insight, encouragement, and understanding along your journey of self-discovery.

Incorporating these journaling prompts into your daily routine can enhance self-awareness, promote emotional healing, and strengthen your relationship with yourself. Through introspective writing, you can navigate the depths of your inner world, uncover hidden truths, and embark on a transformative journey toward self-love. Remember that journaling is a personal practice tailored to your unique needs and experiences—embrace it as a safe space for exploration and growth.

Mindfulness exercises are a powerful way to cultivate a present and compassionate attitude towards oneself. By grounding oneself in the present moment, individuals can learn to observe their thoughts and emotions without judgment, fostering self-awareness and self-compassion. Mindfulness is about being fully present in the moment, acknowledging one's feelings and thoughts without getting caught up in them.

One effective mindfulness practice is deep breathing. Taking a few moments each day to focus on your breath can help calm the mind, reduce stress, and increase self-awareness. Simply close your eyes, take a deep breath through your nose, hold it for a moment, and then exhale slowly through your mouth. Repeat this several times, allowing yourself to be fully present with each breath.

Another beneficial mindfulness exercise is body scan meditation. This practice involves mentally scanning your body from head to toe, paying attention to any areas of tension or discomfort. By bringing awareness to physical sensations, individuals can release built-up stress and develop a deeper connection with their bodies. Start at the top of your head and slowly move down through each part of your body, noticing any sensations without judgment.

Gratitude journaling can also be a form of mindfulness that cultivates self-compassion. Taking time each day to write down things you are grateful for can shift your focus towards positivity and abundance. Reflect on moments that brought you joy or appreciation throughout the day, no matter how small they may seem. This practice trains the mind to notice the good in life and fosters a sense of contentment within oneself.

Incorporating mindful walking into your daily routine can further enhance your self-compassion journey. Take a stroll outside, paying attention to each step you take, the sounds around you, and the sensations in your body as you move. Walking mindfully can help quiet the mind, reduce anxiety, and increase feelings of connectedness to yourself and the world around you.

Practicing self-compassion meditation is another impactful way to develop a kinder relationship with oneself. Set aside time each day to sit quietly and offer yourself words of kindness and understanding. Repeat affirmations such as "I am worthy of love and compassion" or "I forgive myself for past mistakes" with sincerity and gentleness.

By incorporating these mindfulness exercises into your daily routine, you can foster a deeper sense of self-compassion and cultivate a loving mindset towards yourself. Remember that self-care is not selfish but essential for overall well-being and personal growth. Take small steps daily to nurture yourself with kindness and compassion, knowing you deserve love just as much as anyone else.

Embracing daily affirmations, journaling, and mindfulness exercises is more than a routine; it's a transformative journey toward self-love. These practices are designed to be simple yet profoundly effective in altering how you perceive and treat yourself. By consistently integrating these tools into your daily life, you actively reshape your mental landscape, paving the way for increased self-esteem and a deeper connection with your inner self.

Affirmations and positive self-talk are powerful antidotes to the often-unnoticed negative chatter that can dominate our thoughts. Replacing harmful narratives with uplifting and supportive messages directly impacts your emotional well-being, making you more resilient against life's challenges. Think of these affirmations as seeds of positivity that, when nurtured daily, bloom into a garden of self-acceptance and confidence.

Journaling is about recording events and exploring and resolving complex feelings. This practice offers a safe haven to confront fears, celebrate successes, and acknowledge growth. Putting pen to paper provides clarity and continuity in your journey of self-discovery, helping you understand and appreciate who you truly are.

Mindfulness brings you back to the present moment, away from the regrets of the past or anxieties about the future. It cultivates a compassionate attitude toward yourself, teaching you to experience life without harsh judgment or criticism. Through mindfulness, you learn the art of being present - not just as an observer but as an active participant in your life.

Remember, each step in this process is a step towards loving yourself more fully. The path to self-love requires commitment and patience; however, the benefits are immeasurable. You have the power to redefine your relationship with yourself. Start small if you need to—perhaps with a single affirmation each day, a few lines in a journal each week, or a minute of mindfulness each morning.

As you continue on this path, encourage yourself just as you would encourage a dear friend. Celebrate your efforts because each moment spent on these practices is an investment in your well-being and happiness. Let these tools guide you to the love you deserve—love that emanates from within and transforms every aspect of your life.

Chapter 8: Resilience: The Art of Bouncing Back with Love

"Forgive yourself for not knowing what you

didn't know before you learned it."

Maya Angelou

Can You Bounce Back with Love?

Resilience is not just about getting back on your feet. It's about doing so with a heart full of compassion, especially towards oneself. In the journey of self-acceptance, resilience emerges as a cornerstone, enabling individuals to face setbacks without being ensnared by self-doubt. This chapter delves into how resilience can transform not just moments of failure but our entire approach to self-love and acceptance.

Building resilience is essential; it is a buffer against the harshness of life's challenges. When we talk about resilience in the context of self-love, it's not merely about enduring hardship but also about managing these situations with self-compassion and grace. This approach helps maintain a positive self-image even when external circumstances are less than favourable.

The first key lesson here is understanding the role of resilience in overcoming setbacks. It's about more than survival; it's about thriving with a kind heart towards oneself. By fostering resilience, you equip yourself to navigate life's ups and downs without losing your self-worth or love.

Next, we explore practical strategies to strengthen emotional resilience. This includes establishing healthy boundaries, practicing mindfulness, and developing a supportive network. These tools help cushion the blow when we stumble and remain steadfast in our love for ourselves through those turbulent times.

A crucial aspect often overlooked is celebrating progress and learning from failures without self-judgment. This involves shifting perspectives from viewing failures as catastrophes to seeing them as opportunities for growth and learning. Such a shift is vital for maintaining a resilient mindset and fostering continuous self-improvement.

Furthermore, this chapter provides actionable advice to incorporate into your daily routine to bolster your emotional defenses. From simple affirmations that reaffirm your worth to journaling exercises that enhance self-awareness, these small yet impactful actions can pave the way for substantial changes in how you perceive and react to challenges.

Moreover, by embracing resilience, you're not just surviving; you're allowing yourself to thrive in adversity while nurturing the love you have for yourself. It's about turning every setback into a setup for a comeback rooted in love and acceptance.

Through engaging narratives and real-life examples, this chapter instructs and inspires. It encourages you to consider resilience a skill and an essential component of your journey towards unconditional self-love. Here, you learn that every challenge is an invitation to strengthen your relationship with yourself—turning every obstacle into an opportunity for personal growth and more profound self-acceptance.

By the end of this chapter, equipped with knowledge and practical strategies, you will be more prepared to face life's uncertainties with confidence and compassion—knowing well that each step back can be a dynamic leap forward in your journey toward loving yourself completely.

Resilience is the cornerstone of navigating life's challenges with grace and self-compassion. It protects against the storms of setbacks and failures, allowing us to bounce back stronger and wiser. Developing resilience is not about avoiding difficulties but facing them head-on with a mindset of growth and self-acceptance. It enables us to weather the toughest times without self-doubt or criticism. Resilience is not just about surviving; it's about thriving despite adversity.

In times of adversity, it's easy to fall into patterns of self-blame or doubt. However, resilience empowers us to approach setbacks with a sense of self-compassion. By acknowledging our struggles without judgment and extending kindness towards ourselves, we can cultivate a deep well of inner strength. This strength allows us to persevere in the face of challenges, knowing we can overcome whatever comes our way.

Resilience is not reserved for a select few; it is a skill that can be nurtured and developed over time. By actively working on building our resilience, we equip ourselves with the tools necessary to navigate life's ups and downs with courage and fortitude. Every setback becomes an opportunity for growth, and every failure is a stepping stone toward success. Embracing resilience means embracing the belief that we can overcome any obstacle that stands in our way.

Self-compassion plays a crucial role in fostering resilience. When we treat ourselves with kindness and understanding, we create a solid foundation upon which our resilience can thrive. Instead of harsh self-criticism, we offer encouragement and support, nurturing our inner strength and resolve. Through self-compassion, we learn to see setbacks not as reflections of our worth but as opportunities for growth and learning.

Embrace Your Setbacks as Stepping Stones Toward Resilience and Self-Compassion

Resilience is not about avoiding challenges but facing them head-on with courage and compassion. Building resilience is key to navigating setbacks with grace and perseverance in the journey towards self-love. In the next section, let's explore practical strategies to strengthen our emotional resilience and maintain self-love during life's trials.

Emotional resilience becomes our greatest ally in maintaining self-love in times of challenge and adversity. Strengthening emotional resilience involves developing strategies that can help us weather the storms of life while still holding onto our sense of self-worth and compassion. One essential strategy is practicing self-care, which involves setting aside time for activities that rejuvenate and nourish our minds, bodies, and spirits. Whether taking a walk in nature, meditating, or enjoying a warm bath, self-care is a powerful tool for replenishing our emotional reserves and building resilience.

Another crucial aspect of enhancing emotional resilience is cultivating a strong support network. Surrounding ourselves with understanding and compassionate individuals can give us the encouragement and validation we need during tough times. When overwhelmed or distressed, we must contact friends, family members, or support groups. Sharing our struggles with others lightens the emotional burden and reinforces that we are not alone in our challenges.

Setting realistic goals is also key to bolstering emotional resilience. We can prevent feeling overwhelmed or defeated by breaking down larger objectives into smaller, manageable tasks. Celebrating each small victory can boost our confidence and motivation to keep moving forward, even when faced with obstacles.

In moments of adversity, it's common to experience various emotions, including **fear**, **anxiety**, or **sadness**. Acknowledging these emotions without judgment is vital in maintaining emotional resilience. Practicing self-compassion involves treating ourselves with kindness and understanding, much like we would comfort a friend going through a tough time. This gentle approach to self-talk can help us navigate challenges with greater ease and prevent negative self-perception from taking hold.

Moreover, embracing flexibility in our thinking can contribute significantly to our emotional resilience. Life is unpredictable, and setbacks are inevitable. Instead of rigidly clinging to specific outcomes or expectations, adapting to changing circumstances can help us bounce back more effectively when faced with challenges. Flexibility allows us to adjust our strategies, explore new possibilities, and find alternative solutions to obstacles that may arise along the way.

Remember that building emotional resilience is a journey rather than a destination. By incorporating these strategies into your daily life and consistently practicing self-compassion and flexibility, you can cultivate a strong foundation for navigating challenges while maintaining your sense of self-worth and love. Stay committed to your growth and well-being, knowing that each step you take towards strengthening your emotional resilience brings you closer to embracing the love you deserve.

Resilience-Building Framework: R.A.L.M.

The resilience-building model, R.A.L.M., is a structured approach designed to assist individuals in cultivating emotional resilience, a crucial element in the journey toward self-love. This four-step model focuses on recognizing emotions, accepting reality, learning from experience, and moving forward. Each step empowers individuals to navigate setbacks with grace and self-compassion, fostering growth and self-acceptance.

Recognizing Emotions

In the first step of the R.A.L.M. model, *recognizing emotions*, individuals are encouraged to identify and acknowledge their feelings without judgment. This step emphasizes the importance of self-awareness in building resilience. By recognizing their feelings, individuals can gain insight into their reactions to challenges, paving the way for a deeper understanding of themselves and their triggers. Practicing mindfulness and reflective journaling can aid in this process, allowing individuals to observe their emotions without getting entangled.

Accepting Reality

The second step, accepting reality, involves coming to terms with the situation, no matter how challenging it may be. It requires individuals to acknowledge what is within their control to change and what is beyond their influence. By accepting reality, individuals can effectively focus on actionable steps to address the setback. This step encourages a mindset shift towards problem-solving and resilience-building rather than dwelling on what cannot be changed.

Learning from Experience

Learning from experience, the third step in the model prompts individuals to extract valuable lessons from setbacks or failures. This involves reflecting on the experience, identifying strengths and weaknesses, and understanding how these insights can contribute to personal growth. By viewing setbacks as opportunities for learning and development, individuals can reframe their perspective on challenges, turning them into stepping stones towards self-improvement.

Moving Forward

The final step of the R.A.L.M. model is moving forward. This step focuses on applying the lessons from the setback to take constructive action toward recovery and growth. By integrating newfound insights into their approach, individuals can make informed decisions that align with their values and aspirations. Moving forward involves setting goals, creating action plans, and implementing strategies that support personal development and resilience.

Following the R.A.L.M. framework, individuals can navigate setbacks with resilience and self-compassion, fostering a sense of empowerment and self-love. Each step builds upon the other, creating a holistic approach to overcoming challenges with grace and learning from adversity without self-judgment or criticism. The model provides a roadmap for personal growth and emotional mastery, guiding individuals toward a more resilient and self-loving mindset.

Resilience is not just a tool for survival; it's a fundamental component of cultivating deep, enduring self-love and compassion. Throughout this discussion, we've explored the pivotal role of resilience in handling life's inevitable setbacks with grace and maintaining self-love even in the face of challenges. Remember, resilience empowers you to embrace each experience as an opportunity for growth and self-discovery.

One crucial takeaway is the importance of developing strategies that reinforce emotional resilience. By prioritizing practices like mindfulness, setting realistic expectations, and seeking supportive relationships, you can fortify your emotional defenses against adversity. These strategies help you bounce back and ensure you're moving forward stronger and more integrated.

Celebrating your progress and learning from failures without judgment is essential. This approach fosters a healthy perspective where every step forward counts, regardless of its size. It's vital to recognize that setbacks are not reflections of failure but stepping stones toward greater emotional strength and personal insight.

As you move forward, carry with you the understanding that resilience is a dynamic skill that can be nurtured and strengthened over time. Each challenge faced with a resilient spirit adds to your ability to cope and deepens your capacity for self-love. By adopting these principles into your daily life, you'll be capable of overcoming hardships and thriving amidst them.

Embrace these insights and actively integrate them into your journey towards self-acceptance. The path might be challenging, but equipped with resilience, each step becomes a testament to your commitment to fostering unshakable self-love.

Chapter 9: Setting and Achieving Self-Love Goals: Aligning with Your Values

"You yourself, as much as anybody in the entire universe,

deserve your love and affection."

Buddha

Unravel the Threads of Self-Doubt: Weave a New Tapestry of Self-Love

The most formidable obstacles often lie in our minds in the journey towards self-acceptance. Negative self-talk and limiting beliefs erode our self-worth and skew our perception of what we can achieve. The essential first step in transforming this inner dialogue is mastering techniques to overcome these mental barriers. This process is not about silencing your inner critic entirely but transforming its message to serve rather than hinder you.

Setting goals that resonate deeply with personal values marks a significant phase in nurturing self-love. It's about aligning aspirations with actions, ensuring every step is toward the truest version of oneself. However, setting these goals is just the beginning. The real challenge—and opportunity—lies in pursuing these goals persistently and measuring progress by achievements and the growth experienced along the way.

The celebration of small victories plays a crucial role in sustaining motivation throughout this journey. Each achievement, no matter how minor it may seem, is a testament to your commitment to self-love and deserves recognition. This practice not only reinforces positive behaviours but also helps in building a resilient and compassionate self-image.

Step-by-Step Guide: Crafting Your Self-Love Blueprint

Step 1: Identify Limiting Beliefs

Start by pinpointing the negative beliefs that cloud your self-perception. Challenge these thoughts and replace them with affirmations that empower and uplift you. This shift is fundamental in laying a solid foundation for your journey towards self-love.

Step 2: Set Self-Love Goals

Craft goals that reflect your values and what you aspire to be. Employ the SMART criteria to ensure these objectives are clear and reachable within a reasonable timeframe.

Step 3: Break Goals into Actionable Steps

Decompose your broader goals into manageable, actionable steps. This approach helps maintain clarity and focus, making the journey less daunting and more achievable.

Step 4: Create a Self-Love Action Plan

Outline daily practices that support your self-love goals. Include activities that nourish your body and mind, such as meditation, journaling, or hobbies that bring you joy.

Step 5: Track Your Progress

Maintain a log of your progress. This could be through journal entries or digital apps designed for habit tracking. Seeing your progress visually can be incredibly motivating.

Step 6: Celebrate Achievements

Acknowledge every success along your path. Celebrating achievements reinforces positive behavior and boosts your morale to continue striving forward.

Step 7: Adjust and Refine

Regularly evaluate your strategy and make necessary adjustments to align with your evolving needs and circumstances.

Step 8: Practice Self-Reflection

Engage in periodic reflection to gain deeper insights into your growth and areas needing attention. Honest self-reflection fosters greater self-awareness and enhances decision-making.

Step 9: Seek Support and Accountability

Lean on a supportive community or trusted individuals who

encourage your growth. Sharing your journey can provide additional motivation and invaluable feedback.

Step 10: Stay Committed and Persistent

Persistence is key in any aspect of personal development. Remain committed to your self-love goals despite challenges, using setbacks as stepping stones to greater resilience.

This structured approach provides a roadmap and embeds flexibility, allowing for personal adjustments as required by changing life scenarios. By following these steps diligently, you cultivate an environment where self-love can thrive, transforming how you view yourself and interact with the world around you.

Negative self-talk and limiting beliefs can hinder cultivating self-love and acceptance. These internal dialogues often stem from past experiences, societal influences, or comparisons, leading individuals to doubt their worth and abilities. Overcoming these patterns requires consciously challenging and reframing these thoughts into more empowering narratives. One effective technique is cognitive restructuring, which involves identifying negative thoughts, evaluating their accuracy, and replacing them with more realistic and compassionate alternatives.

By practicing self-compassion and treating oneself with the same kindness and understanding offered to a friend facing similar challenges, individuals can begin to shift their perspective towards self-love. Acknowledging that everyone makes mistakes, faces obstacles, and experiences setbacks is crucial in fostering a sense of common humanity and reducing self-criticism. Self-compassion encourages individuals to embrace their imperfections as part of the shared human experience, promoting resilience and self-acceptance.

Another valuable strategy for combating negative self-talk is positive affirmations. Individuals can gradually rewire their thought patterns toward self-empowerment by intentionally choosing uplifting statements that affirm their worth, capabilities, and potential. Regularly repeating affirmations such as "I am worthy of love and respect" or "I believe in my ability to overcome challenges" can reinforce positive self-perceptions and diminish the impact of critical inner voices.

Mindfulness practices also play a pivotal role in managing negative self-talk and limiting beliefs. Individuals can observe their thoughts objectively and detach from unhelpful narratives by cultivating present-moment awareness without judgment. Mindfulness allows for greater clarity and emotional regulation, enabling individuals to respond to negative thoughts with compassion rather than harsh judgment.

Moreover, seeking support from trusted individuals, such as friends, family members, or mental health professionals, can provide valuable perspectives and encouragement in challenging negative self-perceptions. Sharing one's struggles openly and receiving validation from others can foster a sense of connection and belonging, reinforcing the belief that everyone deserves love and acceptance.

By implementing these techniques consistently and compassionately confronting negative self-talk, individuals can lay the groundwork for developing a healthier self-image rooted in self-love.

Nurturing Self-Love Through Goal Setting and Celebration

Setting and achieving self-love goals is pivotal in aligning with your values and fostering a sense of self-worth. You can embark on a journey toward personal growth and fulfilment by defining clear objectives that resonate with your true self. To begin, reflect on what truly matters to you and what brings you joy and purpose. Consider your core values and aspirations, allowing them to guide you in setting meaningful goals that align with who you are at your essence.

Start by breaking down your goals into manageable steps that are realistic and achievable. This approach prevents overwhelm and provides a clear roadmap for progress. Small, consistent actions towards your goals can lead to significant changes over time, reinforcing your belief in yourself and your capabilities. Remember, progress is progress, no matter how small the steps seem.

Incorporate self-compassion into your goal-setting process. Be kind to yourself if setbacks occur or progress is slower than expected. Self-love involves nurturing yourself through challenges and setbacks and acknowledging that growth is often accompanied by obstacles. Embrace the journey as an opportunity for learning and development rather than viewing setbacks as failures.

Stay connected to your why. Understanding the deeper reasons behind your goals can provide motivation during challenging times. When you feel demotivated or uncertain, revisit the core values driving your aspirations. Remind yourself of the positive impact of achieving these goals on your life and well-being.

Celebrate your progress along the way. Acknowledge even the smallest victories as they signal a movement toward your desired outcome. Recognizing and celebrating achievements reinforce positive behaviour and cultivate a sense of accomplishment.

Share your successes with supportive individuals who uplift and encourage you to self-love.

Regularly reassess and realign your goals with changes in your values or priorities. As you evolve and grow, your aspirations may shift accordingly. Stay attuned to these changes and adjust your goals to ensure they continue to reflect who you are and what you aspire to become.

Engage in practices that nurture self-acceptance alongside goal pursuit. Cultivate habits that promote self-care, mindfulness, and gratitude to sustain a healthy relationship with yourself throughout the goal-setting process. Remember that self-love is not just about achieving external milestones but also about honouring and caring for yourself along the way.

Setting and achieving self-love goals that resonate with your values is a transformative process that empowers you to live authentically and purposefully. By embracing this journey with compassion, resilience, and determination, you pave the way for a life filled with fulfilment, self-acceptance, and unwavering love for yourself.

Pursuing self-love, maintaining motivation, and celebrating achievements are crucial in reinforcing a positive self-image. Cultivating practices that sustain one's commitment to personal growth and acknowledging the milestones achieved along the way are essential. Consistency in nurturing self-love is key to long-term success. To stay motivated and engaged in this transformative journey, it is vital to adopt strategies that support continuous progress and celebrate every step forward.

Setting realistic goals aligned with personal values is fundamental to staying motivated on the path to self-love. Individuals can establish a sense of purpose and direction by defining clear objectives that resonate with one's authentic self. Reflecting on these goals regularly can help track progress and maintain focus, serving as a reminder of the journey's significance. When goals are in harmony with one's values, they become more meaningful and rewarding, fueling motivation to persist even during challenging times.

Establishing a support system can also be instrumental in maintaining motivation on the road to self-love. Surrounding oneself with individuals who uplift, encourage, and believe in one's potential can provide invaluable emotional reinforcement. Sharing achievements with trusted friends or family members can amplify feelings of accomplishment and strengthen one's resolve to continue investing in self-care and personal growth.

Acknowledging and celebrating milestones is a powerful way to boost motivation and reinforce self-worth. Recognizing even the smallest victories cultivates a positive mindset and encourages further progress. Individuals affirm their capabilities and resilience by celebrating achievements and nurturing a sense of pride in their accomplishments. Small victories serve as stepping stones toward larger goals, highlighting the progress toward self-love.

Practicing self-compassion is essential when facing setbacks or challenges along the way. Embracing moments of difficulty with kindness and understanding allows for growth and learning from experiences. Self-compassion enables individuals to navigate obstacles without harsh self-criticism, fostering resilience and perseverance in adversity.

Incorporating self-care routines into daily life can also contribute to maintaining motivation on the path to self-love. Prioritizing activities that nourish the mind, body, and soul reinforces a sense of worthiness and promotes overall well-being. Engaging in practices that bring joy, relaxation, and rejuvenation can replenish energy levels and enhance motivation to continue investing in oneself.

By implementing these strategies for maintaining motivation and celebrating achievements, individuals can cultivate a strong foundation of self-love rooted in resilience, compassion, and purpose. Consistent effort, supported by a nurturing environment and a focus on personal growth, paves the way for lasting transformation and an unwavering belief in one's inherent worthiness.

As we reflect on the strategies discussed, remember that the journey to self-love begins with silencing negative self-talk and dismantling limiting beliefs. Recognizing these internal barriers as the first step toward fostering a profound sense of self-worth is vital. Each time you challenge a critical inner voice, you defend your intrinsic value and pave the way for personal growth.

Setting personal goals that align with your true values is equally crucial. These goals act as beacons, guiding you through life's challenges and focusing your energies on what truly matters. You cultivate an authentic and fulfilling life by ensuring these objectives resonate with your core beliefs. This alignment brings clarity, reducing the noise of everyday pressures and enhancing your commitment to self-care.

Maintaining motivation might seem daunting, but it's achievable through consistent action and celebrating small victories. Recognizing every step forward in this journey reinforces your achievements and bolsters your resolve. Whether small daily affirmations or significant milestones, each deserves recognition and celebration.

Embrace these practices with patience and kindness toward yourself. Remember, the path to self-love isn't about perfection but progress and perseverance. Each effort you make is a testament to your resilience and commitment to living a life that honors your worth.

Take control of your narrative by actively engaging with these techniques. Start today by identifying one limiting belief to challenge or one small goal that reflects your deepest values. Small steps lead to significant changes, and each step forward is an act of love towards yourself.

This journey is yours, and while it requires effort, it promises a rewarding transformation—towards embracing the love you truly deserve.

Chapter 10: The Lifelong Commitment: Nurturing Self-Love Every Day

"The greatest act of courage is not an act of war,

but the act of forgiveness."

Oprah Winfrey

Every Day is a Step Forward: Embrace the Journey of Self-Love

Self-love is not a destination but a journey that unfolds daily. Many believe that achieving self-love is a one-time event marked by a sudden burst of self-awareness and happiness. However, true self-love requires ongoing effort and attention. It demands **patience, dedication, and self-compassion**—qualities that must be nurtured continuously to maintain a healthy relationship with oneself.

In this exploration, we delve into acknowledging the continuous nature of self-love. Just as any meaningful relationship in your life requires care and attention, so does your relationship with yourself. This chapter offers practical strategies and insights to help you cultivate a loving relationship with yourself daily, turning self-care into a habitual act rather than an occasional treat.

Understanding the need for patience in your journey is crucial. Self-love grows over time and can't be rushed. It evolves through experiences, challenges, and reflections. Similarly, dedication is key; setting aside time regularly for self-care activities that nourish your body and mind is essential. Lastly, practicing self-compassion means being kind to yourself in moments of failure or disappointment rather than overly critical or harsh.

To integrate these concepts into daily life, developing personalized routines and rituals promoting ongoing self-care is beneficial. These might include setting aside time each morning to meditate, keeping a gratitude journal, or engaging in regular physical activity that you enjoy. The idea is to create routines that feel less like chores and more like cherished parts of your day.

Moreover, dealing with setbacks is an inevitable part of any journey. Implementing strategies to handle these moments constructively can prevent them from derailing your progress toward self-love. Techniques such as mindful breathing to manage stress on the spot or having pre-planned affirmations can help maintain your focus on self-compassion.

Encouragement plays a vital role, too. Remind yourself often that the path to loving yourself is not linear. Each day presents new challenges and opportunities for growth. By adopting a proactive approach to self-love, you empower yourself to take control of your emotional well-being.

Remember, embracing self-love as a lifelong commitment leads to profound rewards. It enhances your resilience, boosts your confidence, and improves overall happiness. So start today; dedicate this moment—and every moment hereafter—to nurturing the love you truly deserve.

Self-love is a lifelong commitment that requires patience, dedication, and self-compassion. It's essential to understand that the journey toward self-love is not a quick fix but an ongoing process that demands continuous nurturing and care. Patience is key in this journey, as it allows us to give ourselves the time needed to grow, heal, and flourish. We must be patient with ourselves as we navigate the ups and downs of self-discovery and self-acceptance.

Dedication plays a crucial role in nurturing self-love every day. By committing to practices that promote self-care and self-compassion, we reinforce our worth and prioritize our well-being. Dedication involves showing up for ourselves consistently, even when it's challenging or when setbacks occur. It's about making a conscious choice daily to prioritize our mental, emotional, and physical health.

Self-compassion is the cornerstone of the self-love journey. It involves treating ourselves with the same kindness and understanding that we would offer to a friend facing a difficult situation. Self-compassion allows us to acknowledge our imperfections and mistakes without judgment or harsh criticism. It enables us to embrace our humanity fully and with grace, fostering a sense of warmth and acceptance towards ourselves.

In moments of doubt or struggle, practicing self-compassion can be incredibly empowering. Instead of berating ourselves for perceived failures or shortcomings, we can offer ourselves encouragement and support. Self-compassion reminds us that we deserve love and forgiveness, even when we stumble.

To sustain a loving relationship with ourselves, we must consistently cultivate these qualities—patience, dedication, and self-compassion. They form the foundation for building a strong sense of self-worth and acceptance. By embracing these principles daily, we create a nurturing environment within ourselves where love can flourish unconditionally.

Embracing patience, dedication, and self-compassion in your self-love journey will pave the way for lasting growth and transformation.

Cultivating Daily Self-Love Through Personalized Routines and Resilience

Developing personalized routines and rituals that promote ongoing self-care and love is crucial in nurturing daily self-love. Creating a daily self-care plan tailored to your needs can significantly impact your well-being and self-esteem. Start by identifying activities that bring you joy, peace, and relaxation. This could include meditation, journaling, reading, exercise, or any other activity that resonates with you. Incorporating these activities into your daily routine can help you prioritize yourself and cultivate a loving relationship with your mind and body.

Setting boundaries is another essential aspect of practicing self-love. Learn to say no to things that drain your energy or do not align with your values. Establishing healthy boundaries protects your emotional well-being and shows you the respect you deserve. This might involve limiting time spent on social media, saying no to additional commitments, or creating space for solitude when needed.

Expressing gratitude is a powerful way to cultivate self-love daily. Take a few moments each day to reflect on what you are grateful for, big or small. This practice can shift your focus from what is lacking in your life to what brings you joy and fulfilment. Embracing an attitude of gratitude can foster a sense of abundance and contentment within yourself.

Self-compassion plays a significant role in nurturing self-love. Treat yourself with the same kindness and understanding you would offer a friend facing challenges. Acknowledge your mistakes without judgment and learn from them with compassion. Remember that setbacks are a natural part of growth and do not define your worth or capabilities.

Incorporate self-affirmations into your daily routine to reinforce positive beliefs about yourself. Repeat affirmations that resonate with you, such as "I am enough," "I deserve love and respect," or "I am worthy of happiness." By affirming these truths regularly, you strengthen your self-esteem and cultivate a more loving relationship with yourself.

Prioritize self-care practices that nourish your mind, body, and spirit. This could involve getting adequate rest, eating nourishing foods, engaging in physical activity, or indulging in activities that bring you joy. Self-care is not selfish; it is essential for maintaining balance and well-being in all areas of your life.

Finally, create a self-love ritual you can engage in daily or weekly. This could be a dedicated time for reflection, self-care activities, or simply being present with yourself without distractions. Rituals provide structure and consistency, reinforcing the importance of nurturing self-love as an ongoing practice rather than an occasional indulgence.

By developing personalized routines and rituals that promote ongoing self-care and love, you actively invest in your well-being and strengthen your relationship with yourself. These practices lay the foundation for a life filled with self-compassion, resilience, and unshakable self-love.

In the journey of nurturing self-love every day, setbacks are inevitable. It's crucial to have strategies to navigate these challenges while maintaining a loving relationship with oneself. One key strategy is to practice self-compassion. Instead of being hard on yourself when setbacks occur, remind yourself that setbacks are a natural part of growth and learning. Treat yourself with the same kindness and understanding you would offer to a friend facing a similar situation.

Another effective strategy is to focus on gratitude. Take a moment each day to reflect on things you are grateful for, even in the face of setbacks. Gratitude can shift your perspective and help you see the positive aspects of your life, fostering a sense of self-appreciation and love.

Setting boundaries is also essential in maintaining a loving relationship with yourself. Learn to say no to things that drain your energy or do not align with your values. By prioritizing your well-being and needs, you demonstrate self-respect and cultivate a deeper sense of self-love.

Engaging in activities that bring you joy and fulfilment is another powerful way to overcome setbacks and nurture self-love. *Find hobbies or practices that resonate with you*, whether painting, dancing, or spending time in nature. These activities can serve as outlets for self-expression and rejuvenation, helping you stay connected to yourself even during challenging times.

Seeking support from trusted individuals can provide comfort and encouragement when facing setbacks. Share your struggles with someone who uplifts and understands you, whether a friend, family member, or therapist. Connecting with others can remind you that you are not alone in your journey toward self-love.

Practicing mindfulness is a valuable tool for dealing with setbacks and maintaining self-love. Mindfulness involves staying present in the moment without judgment. When faced with challenges, take a few deep breaths and ground yourself in the present reality. This practice can help you respond to setbacks with clarity and compassion.

Lastly, remember that setbacks do not define your worth or progress in cultivating self-love. View them as opportunities for growth and learning, allowing them to deepen your understanding of yourself and strengthen your commitment to self-care. By implementing these strategies, you can navigate setbacks with resilience and continue nurturing a loving relationship with yourself daily.

As we reflect on the journey of self-love, we must recognize that this is not a destination but a continuous path that demands our daily commitment and attention. Patience, dedication, and self-compassion are not just strategies but foundational principles that empower us to maintain a nurturing relationship with ourselves.

Firstly, understanding that setbacks are part of the journey helps us foster **resilience**. Responding with kindness and compassion towards ourselves is crucial when faced with challenges. This isn't merely about feeling better in the moment; it's about building a robust framework for long-term emotional health.

Moreover, establishing personalized routines and rituals is vital. These are not just tasks but are meaningful practices that reinforce our commitment to self-love. Whether starting the day with a few minutes of meditation or ending it with gratitude journaling, these rituals serve as anchors, keeping us connected to our core values and goals.

It's also important to remember that you can shape your emotional well-being. Engaging actively with the strategies discussed empowers you to build a more loving and forgiving relationship with yourself. Each small step you take is a significant leap toward transforming self-doubt into self-acceptance.

Remember, every day presents a new opportunity to practice self-love. By engaging in this ongoing process, you are affirming your worth and potential. Let each day be a step forward in embracing the love you truly deserve.

Chapter 11: Customizing Your Self-Love Plan: A Tailored Approach

"Self-love is an ocean and your heart is a vessel. Make it full,

and any excess will spill over into the lives

of the people you hold dear. But you

must come first."

Beau Taplin

Tailor Your Path to Unshakeable Self-Love

Creating a personalized self-love plan isn't just beneficial; it's essential for anyone looking to transform self-doubt into self-acceptance. Each individual faces unique challenges and harbours different dreams, making a one-size-fits-all approach to self-love inadequate. This chapter delves into the nuances of designing a self-love strategy that mirrors your personal journey, acknowledging that the effectiveness of such plans hinges on their customization.

Understanding your unique needs is the first step in crafting a plan that will resonate with you and be sustainable in the long run. It's vital to assess where you stand with your self-esteem and pinpoint the specific areas that need nurturing. This tailored approach allows you to focus on strategies that address your personal obstacles and leverage your strengths rather than wasting effort on generic advice that may not apply to your situation.

Adjusting your self-love practices as your life evolves is another crucial aspect. Life is dynamic, and our emotional needs shift as our circumstances change. What works for you today might not be as effective tomorrow. Therefore, flexibility in your self-love plan is key. This adaptability ensures that you are always supported, regardless of life's unpredictabilities, and fosters continuous growth towards more profound self-acceptance.

Regularly reviewing and updating your self-love plan is equally essential. This isn't just about making minor tweaks; it's about reflecting on your growth and re-aligning your strategies with your current goals and challenges. Ongoing evaluation helps keep your approach fresh and relevant, ensuring you are always moving forward, not just running in place.

The concept of a customized plan also empowers you to take control of your journey towards self-love. By actively creating and adjusting this plan, you reinforce the belief in your ability to manage and improve your emotional health. This proactive stance is fundamental in transforming your views and increasing your resilience against self-doubt.

Moreover, adopting a tailored approach makes you more likely to stick with the plan because it feels more relevant and less like a chore. When actions feel personal and impactful, motivation naturally follows. This connection fosters a deeper commitment to the practices that nourish your well-being and accelerate your path to genuine self-acceptance.

Crafting a personalized self-love plan is pivotal to nurturing a deeper sense of self-acceptance and compassion. Each individual's journey toward self-love is unique and influenced by personal experiences, challenges, and aspirations. One can pave the way for a more impactful and sustainable self-care practice by tailoring a self-love plan to address specific needs and obstacles.

- **Understanding Your Needs:** Begin by reflecting on your own needs and desires. What areas of your life require more attention and care? Identifying these aspects can help you prioritize where to focus your self-love efforts. Whether setting boundaries, practicing self-compassion, or cultivating positive affirmations, understanding your needs is the first step towards creating a plan that resonates with you personally.

- **Acknowledging Obstacles:** Recognizing obstacles hindering your journey toward self-love is essential. These obstacles could be internal, such as negative self-talk and limiting beliefs, or external, like toxic relationships or societal pressures. By acknowledging these challenges, you can develop strategies to overcome them and cultivate a more nurturing relationship with yourself.

- **Setting Aspirations:** Define what self-love looks like for you. What are your aspirations when it comes to self-acceptance and well-being? Setting clear goals can provide direction and motivation toward greater self-love. Whether practicing gratitude daily, engaging in activities that bring you joy, or prioritizing self-care, outlining your aspirations can guide your personalized self-love plan.

- **Tailoring Your Practices:** Once you have identified your needs, acknowledged obstacles, and set aspirations, it's time to tailor your self-love practices accordingly.

146

Experiment with journaling, mindfulness exercises, or affirmations to see what resonates most with you. Customizing your approach ensures that your self-love plan is aligned with your preferences and lifestyle.

- **Consistency is Key:** Remember that consistency is key when practicing self-love. Incorporate small rituals into your daily routine that reinforce feelings of worthiness and appreciation for yourself. Whether starting the day with positive affirmations or moments of reflection and gratitude, consistency in these practices can foster a deeper sense of self-love over time.

- **Seek Support:** Don't hesitate to seek support from friends, family, or a therapist on your journey towards self-love. Surrounding yourself with individuals who uplift and encourage you can provide invaluable support as you navigate challenges and celebrate victories. Building a supportive network can enhance the effectiveness of your personalized self-love plan.

Embrace the Power of Personalization

By crafting a personalized self-love plan that addresses your individual needs, obstacles, and aspirations, you are taking proactive steps toward cultivating a more profound sense of self-acceptance and compassion. Tailoring your practices to fit your unique experiences and goals empowers you to embrace self-love in a way that feels authentic and sustainable. Keep exploring different strategies, adjusting as needed, and remember that your journey toward self-love is an ongoing process of growth and discovery.

Adjusting self-love practices to align with changing life circumstances and personal growth is crucial to maintaining a sustainable journey toward self-acceptance. Life is dynamic, and what works for us today may need modifications tomorrow. We must be adaptable and flexible in our self-love routines to ensure they remain effective and relevant as we evolve.

One practical strategy for adjusting self-love practices is regular reflection and assessment. Take time to evaluate how your current self-love routines are serving you. Are there areas that need more attention or improvements? By regularly checking in with yourself, you can identify what is working well and what may need adjustment.

Another helpful approach is to stay attuned to your emotions and needs. Life changes can bring about different emotional states, requiring tailored self-care practices. If you're feeling overwhelmed, stressed, or anxious, adjusting your self-love activities to prioritize relaxation, mindfulness, or stress-reducing techniques can be beneficial.

Embrace the concept of progress over perfection when it comes to self-love practices. Understand that some days will be more challenging, and it's okay not to follow your routine perfectly every day. Grant yourself grace and compassion during times of change or difficulty, knowing that the journey toward self-acceptance is ongoing and doesn't require flawless execution.

As you navigate changing circumstances, remember to be kind to yourself. Self-love isn't about achieving a specific goal or following a rigid plan; it's about nurturing a compassionate relationship with yourself through all life's ups and downs. Practice self-compassion by treating yourself with the kindness you would offer a close friend facing challenges.

Stay open to new self-love practices that resonate with your current needs and growth. Explore techniques like journaling, meditation, creative expression, or physical activities aligning with your evolving self-care requirements. Remaining curious and open-minded can lead to discovering new ways to support your well-being.

Lastly, seek support from trusted friends, family members, or professionals during transition or personal growth. Sharing your journey towards self-acceptance with others can provide valuable insights, encouragement, and accountability. Remember that it's okay to ask for help when needed; vulnerability is a strength that can deepen your connection with yourself and others.

Remember that flexibility and self-compassion are key components of a sustainable journey towards self-acceptance, as well as adapting your self-love practices to fit changing circumstances and personal growth. By embracing the fluidity of life and being gentle with yourself during times of transition, you can cultivate a resilient foundation of self-love that evolves alongside you.

Self-Love Plan Framework: The Compassionate Path

Crafting a personalized self-love plan is a dynamic process that requires regular review and adjustment to ensure its effectiveness and relevance. The Compassionate Path framework offers a structured approach to creating and maintaining a tailored self-love plan that resonates with individual needs, challenges, and aspirations.

Comprehensive Self-Evaluation:

Begin by conducting a thorough self-assessment, considering personal values, sources of joy, current self-care practices, and areas needing improvement. Reflect on what truly matters to you and identify where you derive fulfillment. Acknowledge both strengths and areas for growth with gentleness and compassion.

Prioritizing Self-Love Activities:

Utilize a matrix to prioritize self-love activities based on their impact and the effort required. Identify 'quick wins' that can immediately boost your self-worth alongside longer-term initiatives for sustained self-love. To create a holistic plan, balance activities targeting emotional well-being, physical health, personal growth, and social connections.

Incorporating Activities into Daily Life:

Integrate self-love practices into your daily routine to make them habitual. Schedule time for activities that nurture your well-being, such as meditation, journaling, exercise, or spending time with loved ones. Consistency is key to reinforcing positive habits that support your self-love journey.

Setting Up Feedback Loop:

Establish a feedback loop for yourself by conducting periodic self-assessments to evaluate the effectiveness of your plan. Be open to adjusting your strategies based on evolving needs and circumstances. Flexibility in adapting your plan ensures its continued relevance and impact.

Example Plans and Troubleshooting Tips:

For inspiration, explore example plans tailored to common scenarios or challenges encountered in the self-love journey. Additionally, familiarize yourself with troubleshooting tips for common pitfalls like losing motivation or facing setbacks. These practical strategies will help you navigate obstacles with resilience and perseverance.

The Compassionate Path framework provides a roadmap for creating a sustainable self-love plan that evolves with you. Regularly reviewing and updating your plan ensures it remains effective, meaningful, and aligned with your journey toward unshakable self-acceptance. Embrace the flexibility of this framework as you navigate the twists and turns of your unique path toward greater self-love.

Crafting a self-love plan tailored to your unique circumstances is not just a luxury; it's a necessity for genuine self-acceptance and lasting emotional well-being. By focusing on personalized strategies that address your specific needs, obstacles, and aspirations, you empower yourself to build a more resilient and fulfilling relationship with yourself.

Adjusting your self-love practices as your life evolves is equally crucial. Life is dynamic, and so are you. Embracing flexibility in your self-love plan allows you to respond effectively to changes, ensuring that your practices remain relevant and supportive as you grow and change. This adaptability is key to maintaining a strong foundation of self-love that can withstand the challenges life may throw your way.

Furthermore, the importance of regularly reviewing and updating your self-love plan cannot be overstated. *Continuous evaluation* ensures that each element of your plan remains aligned with your current state of mind and life circumstances. This iterative process not only reinforces your commitment to self-care but also enhances the effectiveness of your efforts towards self-acceptance.

Remember, the goal here is not to follow a static set of rules but to create a living, breathing blueprint that grows with you. This approach ensures that your path always aligns with who you are and who you aspire to be, making the journey towards unshakable self-love not only possible but inevitable.

Take ownership of this process. You have the tools and insight to tailor a plan that reflects and nurtures your individuality. Trust in your ability to adjust and refine this plan over time. With each step forward, you reinforce the belief that you are worthy of love—most notably, from yourself. So keep moving forward, adapting, and growing. Your journey toward deep, enduring self-love is well within reach.

Chapter 12: Dispelling Myths: Understanding True Self-Love

"To be beautiful means to be yourself. You don't need to be

accepted by others. You need to accept yourself."

hich Nhat Hanh

Is It Self-Love or Just Selfishness?

The journey towards genuine self-acceptance often encounters a significant roadblock: misunderstanding what self-love truly entails. Many shy away from embracing self-love, fearing it borders on narcissism or selfishness. This misconception clouds our perception and hinders the path to personal fulfilment and happiness. Self-love, when correctly understood and practiced, is a fundamental component of mental and emotional well-being, not a retreat into egotism.

Self-love is often misinterpreted as putting one's needs and desires above everyone else's at all times, suggesting a disregard for others' feelings or needs. However, this couldn't be further from the truth. Self-love is about balance; it's recognizing your worth and nurturing yourself to be more present and supportive in your relationships with others. It involves setting healthy boundaries, essential for mutual respect in any relationship.

Moreover, addressing these misconceptions head-on lets us clear the air and embrace self-love practices more wholeheartedly. It's crucial to differentiate between self-care and self-absorption. Self-*care* involves activities and practices we engage in regularly to reduce stress and maintain our health and well-being on multiple levels—physical, emotional, spiritual, and mental. On the other hand, self-absorption is an excessive preoccupation with oneself at the expense of others.

Another myth that needs dispelling is the belief that self-love is static—a destination at which, once arrived, no further effort is required. On the contrary, self-love is a dynamic journey. It evolves as we grow and change; it adapts to new life circumstances and challenges. This understanding encourages us to continually invest in personal development and emotional health.

Embracing self-love also lays a solid foundation for lasting happiness and fulfilment. When we understand our intrinsic worth, we are more likely to pursue things that genuinely matter to us and foster relationships that are truly reciprocal and supportive. This alignment of internal values with external actions creates a meaningful and rich life.

In practical terms, fostering self-love can start with small daily affirmations that reinforce positive self-regard or by setting aside time each week for activities that rejuvenate your spirit and body. These acts might seem simple, but they have profound implications for how we view ourselves and interact with the world.

Through this chapter's exploration of what constitutes true self-love versus selfishness, it becomes clear that embracing self-love equips us better to contribute positively to our surroundings. It enhances our capacity to give because we come from a place of fullness rather than scarcity.

By understanding these nuances around self-love, you are empowered to take actionable steps towards nurturing a compassionate relationship with yourself that respects both your needs and those of others around you. This balanced approach enriches your life and the lives of those you interact with, creating a ripple effect of positivity and mutual respect.

Self-love is often misunderstood, clouded by myths that can hinder individuals from fully embracing this crucial aspect of self-care. It's essential to address and debunk these misconceptions to pave the way for a healthier relationship with oneself. One common misconception is that self-love is synonymous with selfishness. Self-love is not about prioritizing oneself at the expense of others but rather about valuing and respecting one's own needs and well-being. It involves setting healthy boundaries, practicing self-compassion, and nurturing oneself to foster growth and fulfillment.

Another myth surrounding self-love is that it equates to arrogance or narcissism. In reality, self-love is about recognizing one's worth without belittling others. It involves acknowledging one's strengths and weaknesses with honesty and compassion, leading to a deeper sense of authenticity and acceptance. Self-love allows individuals to cultivate a positive self-image based on inner qualities rather than external validation, fostering genuine confidence and resilience.

Some may believe that self-love means always feeling happy and confident. However, self-love encompasses embracing all aspects of oneself, including vulnerabilities and insecurities. It involves showing kindness to oneself during challenging times, practicing self-care rituals, and seeking support when needed. Self-love is not about perfection but about embracing imperfections as part of the journey toward growth and self-acceptance.

Moreover, there is a misconception that self-love is selfish or indulgent. On the contrary, self-love is essential for overall well-being. When individuals prioritize their mental, emotional, and physical health, they are better equipped to show up for others authentically and compassionately. Self-love is the foundation for healthy relationships with others, allowing individuals to set boundaries, communicate effectively, and cultivate mutual respect.

Dispelling these myths surrounding self-love is vital in empowering individuals to embark on self-discovery and acceptance. By understanding the true essence of self-love—a practice rooted in compassion, authenticity, and growth—individuals can nurture a deeper connection with themselves and navigate life's challenges with grace and resilience.

Nurturing Self-Love: Understanding the Distinction and Embracing the Journey

Self-love is often misunderstood as selfishness but vital to holistic well-being. Distinguishing between self-love and selfishness is crucial for individuals on the path to embracing their true selves. Self-love entails caring for oneself deeply, respecting one's needs, and nurturing a positive relationship with oneself. It is about recognizing one's worth, acknowledging personal boundaries, and prioritizing inner growth and emotional well-being.

Selfishness, on the other hand, revolves around prioritizing one's needs at the expense of others without regard for their feelings or well-being. It often stems from ego-centric behaviour where only personal desires are considered important. Selfishness disregards the impact of actions on others and lacks empathy or compassion towards those around us.

Understanding the distinction between self-love and selfishness is essential for cultivating healthy relationships with oneself and others. While self-love encourages self-care and emotional nurturing, selfishness promotes a self-centred approach that can lead to isolation and discord in relationships. Self-love focuses on self-compassion, self-acceptance, and personal growth, fostering a positive sense of identity and inner peace.

Practicing self-awareness and mindfulness daily is crucial to fully embrace self-love. We can cultivate a deeper understanding of ourselves and our needs by tuning into our emotions, thoughts, and behaviours. Self-awareness allows us to identify patterns of behaviour that may stem from self-love or selfish tendencies, empowering us to make conscious choices aligned with our values and well-being.

Developing healthy boundaries is another fundamental aspect of distinguishing self-love from selfishness. Setting clear boundaries in relationships helps maintain respect for oneself and others while fostering open communication and mutual understanding. Boundaries safeguard our emotional well-being and ensure we honour our needs without compromising our values or integrity.

True self-love is an act of kindness towards oneself that extends to others through empathy, compassion, and understanding. By recognizing the importance of distinguishing between self-love and selfishness, individuals can nurture healthier relationships with themselves and those around them. Self-love is a foundation for personal growth, emotional resilience, and genuine happiness rooted in acceptance and love for oneself.

Self-love is not merely a concept to aspire to; it is the foundation upon which genuine happiness and a fulfilling life are built. By embracing self-love, individuals equip themselves with the necessary tools to navigate life's challenges with resilience and grace. It is not selfish to prioritize your well-being and happiness; it is essential for leading a balanced and content existence.

Self-love fosters resilience in the face of adversity. When you cultivate a deep sense of love and compassion for yourself, you develop an inner strength that allows you to weather life's storms without losing sight of your worth. Embracing self-love means acknowledging your inherent value and treating yourself with kindness, even when faced with difficulties or setbacks.

Self-love leads to greater fulfilment in all areas of life. When you prioritize your needs and desires, you create a sense of alignment between your actions and values. This alignment brings a profound sense of satisfaction and contentment as you live authentically and in tune with your true self.

Self-love empowers you to set healthy boundaries in relationships. By valuing yourself and recognizing your worth, you establish clear limits on what you will accept from others. This boundary-setting is crucial for maintaining healthy relationships built on mutual respect and understanding.

Self-love enhances self-acceptance by allowing you to embrace all facets of your being, including your strengths and weaknesses. When you love yourself unconditionally, you free yourself from self-criticism and judgment, allowing space for growth and self-improvement without harsh self-condemnation.

Self-love paves the way for authentic joy by enabling you to find happiness within yourself rather than seeking it externally. When you cultivate a deep love and appreciation for who you are, you no longer rely on external validation or material possessions to feel fulfilled.

Embracing self-love is not a luxury; it is a necessity. It is the cornerstone of a fulfilling life, providing the stability and confidence needed to face life's challenges head-on. By prioritizing self-care, setting boundaries, practicing self-compassion, and nurturing a positive relationship with yourself, you pave the way for lasting happiness and well-being. Remember, true happiness begins with loving yourself first.

Understanding and embracing true self-love is fundamental to our holistic well-being. Throughout this discussion, we've tackled common misconceptions that often cloud the true essence of what it means to love oneself. Recognizing these myths as barriers that can prevent us from reaching our full potential in both happiness and fulfilment is crucial.

Self-love is not selfishness. This distinction is vital. Self-love propels us towards personal growth and enhances our ability to contribute positively. It empowers us to stand strong in our values and meet our own needs with the same vigor with which we strive to fulfil the needs of others. By prioritizing our well-being, we are better equipped to support those we care about.

Embracing self-love lays a foundation for genuine happiness and a fulfilling life. It allows us to navigate life's challenges with resilience, maintaining an inner peace that radiates outward. The journey toward self-love requires continuous effort and understanding, but the rewards are immeasurable.

To foster a healthy relationship with oneself, start by practicing self-compassion. Recognize your worth, acknowledge your strengths, and accept your limitations without harsh judgment. Implement small daily affirmations reinforcing your value and slowly transform your critical inner voice into a supportive ally.

Moreover, setting clear boundaries is another practical step towards self-love. It teaches others how to treat us and signals that our needs are valid and important. Boundaries are not barriers; they are the expressions of what we need to thrive.

Finally, remember that self-love is an ongoing process rather than a destination. It evolves as you grow, facing new challenges and milestones. Stay committed to this journey, and know that each step you take builds a stronger, more resilient version of yourself.

By clarifying what self-love truly entails and dispelling myths surrounding it, you can approach these practices with a clearer understanding and deeper commitment. Embrace this path confidently, knowing it leads to a richer, more rewarding life.

Chapter 13: Expert Insights: Powered by Self-Compassion

"The real difficulty is to overcome how you

think about yourself."

Maya Angelou

Why Self-Compassion is Your Greatest Ally in the Journey of Self-Love

Self-love is not just a luxury; it's a fundamental necessity for well-being. Yet, embracing self-love can often seem insurmountable, especially when faced with the relentless demands of daily life and the loud voices of self-doubt. The journey towards transforming these doubts into acceptance is crucial, and expert advice can be your most trusted guide here. This exploration explores how integrating professional insights into your self-love practices can profoundly shift your perspective and catalyze real change.

Psychologists and therapists specializing in self-esteem and self-compassion offer more than just advice; they provide a roadmap for navigating the complex terrain of our inner worlds. By understanding the psychological underpinnings of self-compassion, you can start dismantling the barriers preventing you from appreciating your true self. These experts clarify why we often struggle with self-acceptance and how we can overcome these challenges through evidence-based techniques and strategies.

The power of expert guidance lies in its ability to transform abstract concepts into tangible actions. For instance, learning about the impact of negative self-talk from a cognitive behavioural perspective can motivate you to actively change your internal dialogues. Therapists often use mindfulness and cognitive restructuring techniques to help individuals rewrite their narratives about who they are and what they deserve.

Moreover, self-compassion is linked with numerous psychological benefits, including reduced anxiety, depression, and stress, as well as increased resilience. Understanding these benefits can provide a compelling reason to prioritize self-compassion practices in your daily routine. When you begin to see self-love not just as an act of indulgence but as a vital component of your mental health, it becomes easier to dedicate time and effort to nurture it.

Experts also stress the importance of consistency in practice. Self-loan initiatives are most effective when they are regularly integrated into one's lifestyle rather than seen as a one-off remedy for moments of low confidence. Consistent practice helps build new habits that support a healthier self-image and a more compassionate relationship with oneself.

To enhance these practices further, professionals recommend incorporating specific exercises that foster an environment conducive to growth and healing. Techniques like journaling, guided meditations focused on compassion or structured reflection exercises can be powerful tools in this transformative process.

By adopting these expert-backed strategies, you place yourself on a path filled with growth opportunities—each step driven by understanding and kindness towards yourself. This chapter aims to educate and empower you with practical methods to ensure every moment spent on this journey contributes positively to building unshakable self-love.

Remember, every individual's path to self-love is unique but grounding this journey in expert knowledge ensures that each step is informed, intentional, and incrementally brings you closer to the love you truly deserve. Embrace these insights as your allies; let them guide you through the shadows of doubt towards the light of profound self-acceptance where peace resides within.

Incorporating expert advice and psychological insights into your self-love practices can significantly enhance your journey towards self-compassion and self-acceptance. Professionals specializing in self-esteem and self-compassion can offer valuable perspectives that deepen your understanding of nurturing self-worth. By integrating their guidance, you can gain more insight into the psychological aspects of developing self-compassion.

Experts can provide insights on how to challenge negative self-talk, techniques to cultivate a positive self-image, and strategies to build resilience against inner criticism. Their expertise can illuminate the path toward embracing your true worth and fostering a kinder relationship with yourself.

When you engage with expert recommendations, you open yourself to a wealth of knowledge that complements the self-love exercises in this workbook. Their input enriches your experience by offering evidence-based techniques tailored to support your emotional well-being.

By integrating expert advice, you empower yourself to navigate the complexities of self-compassion with greater clarity and confidence. Their professional insights serve as guiding lights, illuminating the way forward as you work towards embracing a more compassionate view of yourself.

Remember, self-love is a journey; incorporating expert advice can provide essential tools for personal growth. Each piece of guidance acts as a stepping stone, leading you toward a deeper understanding of yourself and fostering a sense of compassion that will transform how you relate to yourself and others.

Elevating Self-Love: The Power of Self-Compassion and Acceptance

Self-compassion and self-acceptance are not just trendy concepts but powerful tools that can transform our inner landscape. Understanding the psychological benefits of embracing these practices is crucial for our well-being. Self-compassion involves treating ourselves with kindness, recognizing our shared humanity, and being mindful of our emotions without judgment. It allows us to acknowledge our struggles without harsh criticism, fostering a sense of warmth and understanding towards ourselves.

When we practice self-compassion, we are more likely to bounce back from setbacks and failures. Research shows that individuals with higher levels of self-compassion experience lower levels of anxiety, depression, and stress. **Self-acceptance** complements self-compassion by encouraging us to embrace all aspects of ourselves, including our imperfections and vulnerabilities. We cultivate a sense of inner peace and authenticity by accepting ourselves unconditionally.

Embracing self-compassion and self-acceptance also enhances our relationships with others. When we are kinder to ourselves, we become more empathetic towards others, fostering deeper connections and understanding. By practicing self-compassion, we create a positive feedback loop that radiates outward, influencing how we engage with the world.

Moreover, self-compassion and self-acceptance play a significant role in boosting our resilience and mental health. They act as buffers against negative self-talk and harmful beliefs, promoting a healthier mindset rooted in self-love and worthiness. Research indicates that individuals who practice self-compassion have higher levels of life satisfaction, optimism, and overall psychological well-being.

It is essential to recognize that self-compassion does not equate to self-indulgence or selfishness; rather, it is about treating ourselves with the same care and understanding that we would offer to a close friend in need. By cultivating these practices, we create a solid foundation for emotional strength and resilience in the face of life's challenges.

Incorporating expert insights into our journey of self-discovery can provide valuable guidance on deepening our practice of self-compassion and self-acceptance. Therapists specializing in these areas can offer tailored strategies and techniques to help us navigate the complexities of our inner world with compassion and grace. By understanding the psychological benefits of these practices, we empower ourselves to embark on a transformative path toward greater self-love and acceptance.

Incorporating evidence-based techniques and expert recommendations can significantly enhance your self-love journey. Integrating these proven strategies into your daily practices can deepen your understanding of self-compassion and self-worth, leading to lasting transformation.

- **Begin with Gratitude:** One powerful technique experts recommend is starting each day with a gratitude

172

practice. Take a few moments in the morning to reflect on what you are thankful for in your life. This simple exercise can shift your focus from what is lacking to what is abundant, fostering a positive mindset that supports self-love.

- **Practice Mindfulness:** Mindfulness exercises can help you become more aware of your thoughts and emotions without judgment. Experts often suggest mindfulness meditation to cultivate self-compassion and promote emotional well-being. By staying present in the moment, you can better understand and respond to your inner experiences with kindness.

- **Challenge Negative Self-Talk:** Experts advise challenging negative self-talk by questioning its validity and replacing it with more realistic and compassionate statements. When you catch yourself engaging in self-criticism, take a moment to reframe those thoughts with kinder words. This practice can help you build a more positive self-image over time.

- **Set Boundaries:** Learning to set boundaries is crucial for cultivating self-love. Experts recommend establishing clear boundaries in your relationships and commitments to protect your emotional well-being. Saying no when necessary and prioritizing your needs can help you create space for self-care and self-compassion.

- **Seek Support:** It's essential to reach out for support when needed. Whether through therapy, support groups, or trusted friends, having a supportive network can bolster your self-love journey. Experts emphasize the importance of seeking professional help if you're struggling with deep-rooted issues that hinder your self-esteem.

- **Practice Self-Care:** Taking care of yourself physically, emotionally, and mentally is fundamental to nurturing self-love. Experts recommend incorporating self-care practices into your routine, such as exercise, healthy eating, adequate sleep, and activities that bring you joy. Prioritizing self-care sends a powerful message of self-worth and importance.

- **Celebrate Your Progress:** Acknowledge and celebrate your progress on your self-love journey. Recognize your efforts, no matter how small they may seem, and celebrate each step forward. By celebrating your achievements along the way, you reinforce positive behaviors and cultivate a sense of pride in your growth.

By implementing these evidence-based techniques and expert recommendations into your daily life, you can enrich your self-love practices and experience profound personal growth.

Remember that self-compassion is a journey—a continuous process of learning, unlearning, and embracing yourself with kindness and understanding.

Embrace Expert Guidance

The journey to self-acceptance and self-love is deeply personal, yet it doesn't have to be navigated alone. Integrating expert advice into your self-love practices enriches your understanding and enhances the effectiveness of each step you take. Professionals in psychology and therapy bring a wealth of knowledge that can illuminate the path to greater self-compassion.

Psychological Benefits are Tangible

Understanding the **psychological benefits** of self-compassion is crucial. It's about recognizing that being kind to yourself is not just a nice-to-have but a fundamental aspect of improving your mental health and overall well-being. Self-compassion fosters resilience, allowing you to recover quickly from setbacks and fully engage in life.

Practical Techniques Make a Difference

Employing evidence-based techniques recommended by experts can significantly boost your progress. These practical strategies are often simple to implement and designed to fit even the busiest schedules. Whether it's mindfulness exercises, journaling, or structured self-reflection, these tools are your allies in building a foundation of robust self-love.

Take action today: Start small if you need to, but start. Each step you take is a piece of the puzzle in understanding yourself better and treating yourself with the compassion you deserve. Remember, the most profound changes often come from consistent, small efforts.

Your ability to master your emotional well-being is within reach. Harness the combined power of expert insights and practical techniques to transform self-doubt into unshakable self-acceptance. You have the strength to overcome challenges; let this knowledge guide you as you continue on your path to the love you truly deserve.

Chapter 14: Cultivating Connection: The Power of Community in Self-Love

"Being different is a revolving door in your life where secure people enter and insecure exit."

Shannon L. Alder

Unveiling the Power of Connectedness in Your Self-Love Journey

In today's digitally-driven world, where isolation often shadows our interactions, the importance of community cannot be overstated—especially on the path to self-love and acceptance. Imagine a supportive network that understands and mirrors your struggles and triumphs in nurturing self-worth. This chapter delves deep into the transformative potential of online communities in bolstering one's journey toward self-acceptance. By engaging with others who share similar challenges, readers can discover a reservoir of motivation and resilience that solo endeavours might rarely tap into.

Community is the cornerstone of sustained self-love. For many, the journey toward self-acceptance begins in solitude but strengthens in solidarity. When individuals come together to share their experiences, they create an echo chamber of empathy and understanding that resonates with each person's struggle against self-doubt and societal pressures. This connection fosters emotional support and practical strategies to overcome common obstacles.

The benefits of such interactions are manifold. Engaging in a community allows you to see the universality of your feelings and experiences, providing a broader perspective that can diminish personal anxieties and enhance self-compassion. It's about transforming the 'me' into 'we,' where personal battles are shared and collective victories are celebrated. This shared journey alleviates the loneliness that often accompanies self-doubt and amplifies the joy of every small win on the path to self-love.

To harness this power, learning how to effectively share your stories of adversity and achievement is crucial. Openness breeds authenticity; being genuine in your communications invites others to respond in kind. This mutual exchange enriches the community experience, creating a safe space where advice is given and received with respect and kindness. It's about building a give-and-take relationship that supports each member's growth.

Using an online platform can significantly enhance this dynamic. Digital communities break geographical barriers and facilitate constant connectivity, ensuring you can seek guidance or offer support whenever needed. Whether posting a query about handling negative self-talk or sharing a personal anecdote of overcoming a difficult day, these platforms provide immediate access to communal wisdom and encouragement.

Moreover, such communities encourage accountability—a key ingredient in maintaining progress on any personal development journey. Knowing that others are watching and cheering you on can be a powerful motivator. It transforms the often daunting road to self-love into a more approachable series of steps, each validated by your peers' encouragement and feedback.

In weaving together these threads of connectivity, empathy, and digital engagement, we find a robust framework for nurturing self-love amidst busy lives filled with external responsibilities. The strategies discussed here are designed to be integrated seamlessly into daily routines, ensuring that even those with limited "me time" can forge meaningful connections that empower their journey toward embracing themselves fully.

This collective approach does not merely supplement the individual pursuit of self-love; it fundamentally reshapes it by embedding each personal story within a tapestry of shared human experience. Herein lies an invaluable lesson: self-love thrives in communion with others. By participating actively in these communities, every individual contributes to a culture of acceptance that uplifts all members.

As we close our exploration into transforming self-doubt into self-acceptance, remember: The path to loving yourself is personal and communal. In connecting with others, we share our own light and reflect back the brilliance we see in those around us—creating a brighter journey for all involved.

Building a supportive community while on a self-love journey can be a transformative experience. Connecting with like-minded individuals striving for self-acceptance can provide a sense of belonging and understanding crucial for personal growth. Through shared experiences, challenges, and successes, individuals can find validation and encouragement, knowing they are not alone in their struggles. This communal support can act as a guiding light, illuminating the path toward self-love and fostering an invaluable sense of connection on this journey.

One of the key benefits of being part of a supportive community is the opportunity to share insights and receive feedback from others. By engaging with peers working towards self-love, individuals can gain new perspectives, learn from different experiences, and expand their understanding of self-acceptance. This exchange of ideas and knowledge can lead to profound personal growth as individuals challenge their beliefs and behaviours in a safe and nurturing environment.

Moreover, being part of a community provides a source of motivation and accountability. When surrounded by individuals committed to their self-love journey, there is a natural inclination to stay focused and dedicated to personal development. The shared commitment to growth can inspire individuals to push past their limitations, overcome obstacles, and strive for continuous improvement in their relationship with themselves.

In addition to motivation, a supportive community offers a space for vulnerability and authenticity. In a world where vulnerability is often perceived as a weakness, having a group of individuals who encourage openness and honesty can be incredibly empowering. By sharing one's struggles and triumphs in a safe environment, individuals can cultivate deeper connections with themselves and others, fostering a sense of self-worth and acceptance that is essential for personal well-being.

Engaging With a Supportive Community Can Provide the Necessary Foundation for Lasting Self-Love

Sharing your experiences, challenges, and successes with others can be a powerful way to foster connection and support on your journey towards self-love. By opening up about your struggles and triumphs, you create a space for authenticity and vulnerability, which can deepen your connections with others navigating similar paths. This sharing is about seeking validation and creating a sense of belonging and understanding. When you express your vulnerabilities, you allow others to see that they are not alone in their struggles, fostering a community of empathy and support.

One practical way to share your experiences is through active participation in online forums or social media groups dedicated to self-love. These platforms provide a safe space for individuals to share their stories, ask for advice, and offer support to one another. Engaging in these communities allows you to receive diverse perspectives and insights, helping you gain new understanding and strategies for cultivating self-love. By actively participating in discussions and sharing your own experiences, you contribute to the collective wisdom of the group.

When sharing your challenges, it's essential to approach them with self-compassion. Rather than viewing setbacks as failures, see them as opportunities for growth and learning. By reframing your challenges in a positive light, you can shift your mindset from one of self-criticism to one of self-compassion. This shift benefits your own mental well-being and sets an example for others in the community, encouraging them to approach their challenges with kindness and understanding.

Celebrating your successes with others is equally important. When you achieve a milestone on your self-love journey, sharing it with the community can be incredibly affirming. Receiving validation and encouragement from others can boost your confidence and motivation, propelling you further toward self-acceptance. Moreover, celebrating your successes inspires others in the community to believe in their ability to overcome obstacles and thrive.

Remember that vulnerability is a strength, not a weakness. By sharing your authentic self with others, you create deeper connections based on mutual understanding and empathy. Embrace the power of community in supporting each other's growth and transformation, knowing that together, you can overcome challenges and celebrate successes on the journey towards unshakable self-love.

In self-love and personal growth, an online platform can be a powerful tool for seeking advice, finding motivation, and enhancing personal development through shared experiences. Utilizing the online community to connect with like-minded individuals can offer a sense of belonging and support in your journey toward self-acceptance. By actively engaging with the platform, you open yourself up to a world of possibilities where you can share your challenges, celebrate your successes, and learn from the diverse experiences of others.

- **Seeking Advice:** One of the most significant benefits of an online community is the ability to seek advice from individuals who have walked similar paths. Don't hesitate to seek guidance when facing obstacles or uncertainties on your self-love journey. By posing questions or sharing your concerns, you invite valuable insights and perspectives that can illuminate new solutions and approaches. Embracing the community's collective wisdom can provide fresh ideas and strategies to navigate challenges effectively.

- **Finding Motivation:** When self-doubt creeps in or motivation wanes, the online platform can inspire inspiration. Engaging with uplifting stories, motivational posts, or encouraging messages from fellow community members can reignite your passion for self-love. Surrounding yourself with positive affirmations and supportive voices can bolster your confidence and remind you of your progress. Harnessing the collective energy of the community can propel you forward on days when staying motivated feels challenging.

- **Enhancing Personal Growth:** Sharing experiences and insights within the online platform benefits you and contributes to the growth of others in the community. By offering your perspectives, lessons learned, and moments of triumph, you inspire those who may be struggling. Embrace vulnerability in sharing your journey, as it fosters connections built on authenticity and mutual understanding. Through this exchange of experiences, giving and receiving support become integral parts of your personal growth trajectory.

Engagement with an online community dedicated to self-love can be a transformative experience, enriching your journey through shared connections and collective wisdom. By actively participating in discussions, offering support to others, and seeking guidance when needed, you contribute to a dynamic ecosystem of empowerment and growth. The power of community lies in its ability to uplift individuals collectively, creating a space where everyone's voice is valued, heard, and respected. Embrace this digital sanctuary as a place where your self-love journey intersects with the journeys of others, forming a tapestry of resilience, compassion, and growth.

Cultivating Connection: The Power of Community in Self-Love

Throughout our exploration of transforming self-doubt into self-acceptance, we've uncovered the undeniable power of community in nurturing and sustaining self-love. By connecting with a supportive network, you not only share your journey but also multiply the joys and the challenges that come with personal growth.

Community is your anchor and springboard—it holds you steady during turbulent times and propels you forward when you're ready to soar. Engaging with others on similar paths allows you to see that your struggles are universal, not solitary.

This realization is vital; it brings comfort and reduces the isolation often accompanying self-doubt.

Sharing experiences serves as a mirror and a window—it reflects your progress and opens up vistas to new strategies and perspectives. Whether it's through celebrating successes or navigating setbacks, these interactions foster resilience and understanding. They remind us that growth is possible, and perfection isn't the goal but authenticity.

Utilizing online platforms can significantly amplify this effect. These digital communities offer continuous accessibility to resources, advice, and motivation that can be tailored to fit into even the busiest schedules. Here, encouragement is just a click away, making it easier to maintain momentum in your self-love journey despite daily pressures.

Let's remember: Every interaction counts. Each conversation and shared story adds layers to our understanding of ourselves and enriches our approach to self-love. By engaging actively with these communities, you harness collective wisdom far greater than what any of us could achieve alone.

As we conclude this exploration into self-love, remember that building connections is not just about finding support—it's about creating it, too. You can contribute positively to others' journeys just as much as they do to yours. This reciprocal relationship enhances individual lives and strengthens the fabric of the community itself.

In embracing these principles, you step into a role where you are both a learner and a mentor, a follower and a leader—positions that are essential for sustained personal development and communal well-being.

So, let's move forward confidently, knowing that we are not alone in our endeavours. Together, in our shared spaces—physical or virtual—we cultivate an environment where self-love thrives through mutual support and collective wisdom. Herein lies our power, resilience, and, ultimately, our success in transforming self-doubt into unshakable self-acceptance.

Embrace this journey fully—connect, share, grow—and watch as the love you deserve unfolds beautifully before you.

Epilogue

"If you want to fly, you must give up

what weighs you down."

Toni Morrison

Stepping Into Your Power: A Journey Concluded, Yet Just Beginning

As we draw the curtains on this transformative journey together, we must pause and reflect on the path we've traversed. From confronting deep-seated self-doubt to unlocking the doors of self-acceptance, you've been equipped with the tools necessary to foster unshakable self-love. But remember, the end of this book is not the end of your journey—it's a beautiful beginning.

The strategies and insights shared here are more than just words on paper; they are practical applications designed for real-world use. Whether you're navigating a demanding career, managing family responsibilities, or juggling both, the techniques we've explored can seamlessly integrate into your daily routine. By setting aside even a few minutes each day for mindfulness or positive affirmations, you can maintain and grow the self-love you've started to cultivate.

Recap of Our Journey Together

Throughout our discussions, we've tackled key areas critical for transforming self-doubt into self-acceptance. We delved into understanding the roots of negative self-talk, learned how to challenge and replace these thoughts with compassion and truth, and explored practical ways to set boundaries that honour your needs and well-being.

To ensure these concepts become a part of your life:

- **Practice mindfulness** regularly to stay connected with your present emotions and thoughts.

- **Employ affirmations** that resonate with your personal truths, reinforcing your worth daily.

- **Schedule 'me-time'** deliberately, making it as non-negotiable as any other appointment.

While this guide has aimed to cover extensive ground in nurturing self-love, it's essential to acknowledge that personal growth is ongoing. There may be areas requiring further exploration or more profound personal adjustment, and that's perfectly okay. The journey of self-love is uniquely yours—ever-evolving as you are.

Take Action: Embrace Your Path

Now is the time to take decisive action. Harness the knowledge and insights from this book not just as fleeting thoughts but as catalysts for real change. Every small step you take builds up like layers of paint on a canvas, eventually revealing a masterpiece—your happiest, most fulfilled self.

As you continue, remember that setbacks and challenges are part of every worthwhile journey. They do not define your worth or the progress you've made. Treat yourself with the kindness and patience you would offer a dear friend because you deserve that love from yourself first and foremost.

Closing Reflection: A Lasting Impression

As we part ways in this written form, I hope that this book's essence lingers in your heart and mind like a gentle but steadfast friend. May you carry the torch of self-love for yourself and as a beacon for others who might be lost in their own shadows of doubt.

"Love yourself first, and everything else falls into line. You

really have to love yourself to get anything

done in this world."

Lucille Ball

Let these words by Lucille Ball remind you daily: loving yourself is not an act of selfishness; it is the foundation upon which all other love builds. Step forward boldly, lovingly, authentically—you deserve nothing less than to be your own greatest ally and friend.

Conclusion

"Self-care is how you take your power back."

Lalah Delia

In conclusion, the journey through these pages has explored the depths of self-love, a subject so intricate yet crucial for our overall well-being. This exploration is about understanding the concept of loving oneself and actively engaging in practices that nurture and affirm this essential aspect of our lives. We've traversed through various landscapes—mindfulness, self-compassion, boundary setting, the impact of external influences, and the power of affirmations—all designed to guide you toward a more loving and compassionate relationship with yourself.

It's essential to remember that self-love is not a static state but a dynamic process that unfolds and deepens over time. Challenges and setbacks are inevitable, serving not as roadblocks but as stepping stones on this path. Each chapter of this narrative has aimed to arm you with the tools and insights necessary to face these challenges with resilience and grace.

- **Mindfulness practices** are at the core of self-love, encouraging a presence that reveals the beauty of the current moment and your place within it.

- **Setting healthy boundaries** is crucial for self-respect and is one of the highest forms of self-love.

- **Navigating external influences** intelligently ensures that you remain true to your authentic self in a world full of noise.

- **Affirmations** serve as powerful reminders of your worth, reinforcing the positive self-image that is your birthright.

- **Self-care** must be understood in its most profound sense—not as an indulgence but as a necessary practice of self-love that entails taking care of your physical, emotional, and spiritual well-being.

Moving forward, it's imperative to approach self-love as a daily commitment rather than a destination to arrive at. It's about making choices that align with your deepest needs and desires, allowing you to live more authentically and fully. Practicing self-love also means granting yourself the permission to evolve, to shed skins that no longer serve you, and to step into new versions of yourself with courage and openness.

Finally, this narrative invites you to consider self-love as an individual pursuit and a collective imperative. In learning to love ourselves, we are better equipped to offer genuine love and support to others, creating ripples of compassion that can transform our communities and, ultimately, our world. The path of self-love is both deeply personal and universally relevant—a beacon of hope and a testament to the human spirit's resilience.

As we close this chapter, remember that the essence of self-love lies within you, waiting to be acknowledged, nurtured, and celebrated. Carry these lessons forward as mere concepts and living practices that animate your daily life. May your journey toward self-love be filled with insight, healing, and the joy of discovering your most authentic self.

Bonus Material

Your Questions, Answered!

1. How do I begin my self-love journey if I struggle with low self-esteem?

Beginning a self-love journey when grappling with low self-esteem might seem daunting, but it's an incredibly worthwhile endeavour. Low self-esteem often stems from a complex mix of past experiences, including criticism from others, perceived failures, or feeling different from those around us. These sources can embed a narrative in our mind that we are not enough, undermining our ability to love and accept ourselves. Therefore, building self-love involves rewriting these narratives and cultivating a kind, compassionate relationship with ourselves.

The first step in this transformative process is to become aware of the critical inner voice perpetuating feelings of inadequacy. This awareness creates a space between the self and the critical thoughts, allowing us to challenge and question their validity. Mindfulness practices can be particularly effective in developing this awareness, as they encourage us to observe our thoughts and feelings without judgment. This observational stance empowers us to kindly redirect our thoughts and cultivate a more supportive and compassionate internal dialogue.

In addition to mindfulness, actively practicing self-compassion can significantly nurture self-esteem. Self-compassion involves treating yourself with the same kindness, concern, and support you would offer a good friend. When faced with challenging moments or perceived shortcomings, responding with compassion rather than self-criticism opens the door to personal growth and self-acceptance. It's about recognizing that imperfection is part of the human experience and allowing yourself room to make mistakes and learn from them.

Further, setting small, achievable goals can foster a sense of accomplishment and build self-confidence. You reinforce your self-worth and capability by focusing on progress rather than perfection and celebrating the small wins along the way. Surrounding yourself with a supportive community that uplifts and values you for who you are can also counteract feelings of isolation and reinforce positive beliefs about yourself.

Ultimately, the path to self-love is unique to each individual and requires patience, persistence, and a willingness to confront uncomfortable truths about ourselves and our past. It's a gradual process of unlearning negative beliefs and replacing them with affirmative ones, honouring our worth and potential. Remember, this journey isn't about reaching a state of perfection; it's about cultivating a lifelong practice of kindness, respect, and love for oneself, even in the face of adversity or doubt.

2. Can mindfulness practices really make a difference in how I view myself?

Mindfulness practices can significantly influence how you view yourself, promoting a more compassionate and accepting self-perception. Mindfulness, in essence, is the practice of being fully present and engaged in the moment without judgment. This simple yet profound state of awareness facilitates a deeper connection with oneself, fostering an environment where self-criticism can give way to a more compassionate and understanding self-dialogue.

Engaging in mindfulness practices teaches us to observe our thoughts and emotions from a place of detachment. Instead of immediately identifying with every thought or feeling as an absolute truth, mindfulness allows us to see them as transient states that come and go. This perspective shift is critical in changing how we view ourselves. For example, instead of getting caught up in a spiral of self-critical thoughts and believing them to be an accurate reflection of our worth, mindfulness invites us to acknowledge these thoughts without letting them define us. We can then consciously direct our focus towards more positive and nurturing thoughts about ourselves.

Furthermore, mindfulness practices cultivate self-compassion, essential for improving self-esteem and self-love. Through mindful breathing, body scans, or loving-kindness meditation, individuals learn to treat themselves with the same kindness and care they would offer to a dear friend. This shift towards self-compassion is vital for challenging and eventually changing the inner narrative, which contributes to low self-esteem. By regularly practicing mindfulness, individuals can develop a more balanced and realistic view of themselves, recognizing their strengths and accepting their weaknesses without overly harsh judgment.

In sum, mindfulness is a tool for breaking the cycle of negative self-perception and building a healthier, more supportive relationship with oneself. By learning to be present with and kind to ourselves, we lay the groundwork for lasting self-esteem and a profound sense of self-love. Over time, mindfulness can transform our relationship with ourselves from one marked by criticism and comparison to one rooted in compassion and acceptance.

3. How can I set healthy boundaries without feeling guilty or selfish?

Setting healthy boundaries is a critical aspect of self-care and personal development, but it can often be accompanied by feelings of guilt or selfishness. This is especially true in cultures that prize selflessness and caring for others, where prioritizing one's own needs is sometimes viewed negatively. But establishing boundaries is neither selfish nor indicative of a lack of caring; instead, it's a vital practice that allows individuals to respect their own needs, limits, and values, fostering a sense of well-being and self-respect.

Firstly, it's important to recognize that setting boundaries is an act of self-respect. It communicates to others how you wish to be treated and what you are and are not comfortable with. This clarity is crucial not just for your well-being but also helps others understand how to interact with you respectfully and respectfully. By setting boundaries, you are taking responsibility for your mental and emotional health and ensuring you are not overextended or taken advantage of. This is essential in all relationships with family, friends, or coworkers.

However, setting these boundaries often triggers guilt because it goes against the grain of wanting to be seen as helpful and accommodating. It's helpful to reframe how you think about boundaries to overcome this. Rather than viewing them as a barrier or a way of pushing others away, consider them as a means of nurturing your relationships by fostering honesty and respect. When clearly communicating your needs and limits, you create a healthier dynamic where both parties feel valued and understood. This shift in perspective can help alleviate feelings of guilt, as you know that setting boundaries is beneficial for you and the health and longevity of your relationships.

Ultimately, feeling guilty or selfish when setting boundaries is a natural reaction for many, but with time, reflection, and practice, these feelings can be managed and even overcome. Remember, setting boundaries is a form of self-love and self-respect, and it is crucial for establishing healthy, balanced relationships. By valuing your needs and openly communicating them, you protect your mental and physical health and contribute to a more honest and respectful interaction with those around you.

4. What specific ways to handle negative external influences, especially on social media?

In today's digitally connected world, social media platforms have become ubiquitous, profoundly influencing our daily lives, perspectives, and self-esteem. While these platforms can offer remarkable opportunities for connection, learning, and entertainment, they also present significant challenges in the form of negative external influences. These can include exposure to unrealistic standards, cyberbullying, and the overwhelming pressure to curate a seemingly perfect life online. Such experiences can lead to feelings of inadequacy, anxiety, and depression, highlighting the need for effective strategies to manage these influences.

To handle negative influences on social media, it's essential to start with self-awareness. This means being mindful of how time spent on these platforms affects your mental and emotional state. Pay attention to feelings that arise after scrolling through your feeds—do you feel uplifted or more self-critical? This awareness can serve as a barometer, guiding you towards healthier online habits. For example, if you notice certain accounts or content types consistently make you feel bad about yourself, consider unfollowing or limiting your exposure to them. Engaging in a digital detox, where you take intentional breaks from social media, can also be a powerful way to reset your mental state and reduce dependency on digital validation.

Furthermore, actively curating your social media feed to include accounts that inspire, educate, and uplift can transform your online experience. Seek out communities and individuals who share positive messages, offer support, and represent a more inclusive and diverse perspective of beauty, success, and happiness. Engaging with content that challenges the narrative of perfection often portrayed online can help recalibrate your understanding of what's real and attainable, counteracting the barrage of negative influences.

Lastly, it's crucial to cultivate a strong support system outside of social media. Meaningful, offline relationships provide a solid foundation of acceptance and understanding, which can buffer the impact of negative online encounters. By investing time and energy in real-world interactions and activities that nurture your well-being, you build resilience against the adverse effects of social media. Remember, while you may not have complete control over what you encounter online, you have the power to choose how you engage with it and protect your mental health in the process.

5. Are there any daily affirmations that can help boost my confidence immediately?

Daily affirmations are short, powerful statements that, when spoken out loud, can help to shift your mindset, reinforce positive thinking, and boost your confidence almost immediately. The practice of using affirmations is based on the principle of neuroplasticity, which suggests that the brain is adaptable and can be rewired through new thoughts and experiences. By repeating positive affirmations, you are effectively training your brain to believe these statements, changing how you think and feel about yourself.

Affirmations work by challenging and overcoming self-sabotaging and negative thoughts. When you repeat them often and genuinely believe in them, you can start making positive life changes. For affirmations to be effective, they must be present tense, positive, personal, and specific. For example, saying "I am confident and capable in my abilities to succeed" directly addresses self-esteem and competence, providing an immediate psychological uplift. By asserting your self-worth, capabilities, or intentions in the present tense, you acknowledge your potential to achieve what you desire, thus fostering a mindset geared towards success and positivity.

Integrating daily affirmations into your routine can be as simple as setting aside a few minutes each morning to voice out or write down affirmations that resonate with your goals and areas in which you seek confidence. This practice sets a positive tone for the day and serves as a foundation for building long-term self-esteem and confidence. Over time, these affirmations can help shift your inner dialogue from doubt and critique to encouragement and self-acceptance, essential for personal growth and resilience.

6. What constitutes self-care beyond the common suggestions of baths and spa days?

Self-care is a multi-dimensional concept that extends far beyond the often-mentioned recommendations of indulging in baths and spa days. While these activities can certainly contribute to one's well-being, self-care encompasses a broader range of practices to nurture mental, emotional, physical, and spiritual health. It involves any deliberate action taken to improve or maintain one's overall state of being, and it's deeply personal, varying significantly from one individual to another.

Self-care is about understanding and attending to your needs, respecting your boundaries, and recognizing when it's time to prioritize your well-being. This might include engaging in regular physical exercise, which benefits both the body and the mind, or ensuring a balanced, nutritious diet to fuel your body adequately. It could also mean practicing mindfulness or meditation to cultivate mental clarity and emotional stability or simply allowing yourself time to rest and recharge without feeling guilty.

Furthermore, self-care involves pursuing hobbies and activities that bring joy and satisfaction, thus helping to alleviate stress and promote a positive mood. It also includes building and maintaining healthy relationships that support and enrich your life while distancing yourself from toxic or draining interactions. On a deeper level, self-care might involve seeking professional help when dealing with mental health issues, such as therapy or counselling, which is a profoundly beneficial and sometimes necessary step in taking care of oneself.

It's essential to recognize that self-care is not a one-time act but a continuous commitment to oneself. It's about making conscious choices daily that align with one's well-being and values rather than an occasional indulgence. By incorporating a range of self-care practices into our lives, we can better manage stress, improve our mental health, and enhance our overall quality of life.

7. How do I maintain a self-love routine during particularly stressful or challenging times?

Maintaining a self-love routine during stressful or challenging times can often seem daunting, yet it's precisely during these periods that such practices are most vital. Stressful situations can drain your physical and emotional energy, weakening your resilience and ability to cope effectively. A self-love routine in these contexts acts as a grounding mechanism, a means to remind yourself of your worth and to nourish your well-being amidst external chaos. It involves intentionally preserving and enhancing your sense of self-worth, self-esteem, and overall mental and physical health. This could range from simple acts of kindness towards yourself and maintaining a healthy lifestyle to seeking professional support when necessary.

Incorporating self-love into your daily life under stress requires adaptability and a gentle approach. It's about acknowledging the current challenges without judgment and understanding that your capacity for self-care might not be the same as it is under less stressful conditions. Identify small, manageable actions that resonate personally and contribute to your well-being. For example, ensuring adequate rest, staying hydrated, and consuming nutritious foods are foundational in managing stress. Similarly, setting aside even a few minutes each day for activities that uplift you, such as reading, meditating, or engaging in a hobby, can significantly impact your emotional health.

Furthermore, practicing self-compassion becomes crucial during challenging times. It's about treating yourself with the same kindness and understanding that you would offer a friend in a similar situation. This may involve reframing negative self-talk into more positive and supportive self-dialogue or simply allowing yourself space and time to feel and express your emotions without guilt. Additionally, recognizing when you need help and reaching out for support, whether from loved ones or professionals, is a profound act of self-love. Maintaining a self-love routine when faced with stress or challenges is not about perfection or a rigorous adherence to a set of practices but rather about making conscious choices to support your well-being amidst life's inevitable ups and downs.

8. Can practicing self-love help improve my relationships with others?

Practicing self-love is a foundational element that significantly influences the quality of our relationships with others. Nurturing a loving and compassionate relationship with ourselves sets the tone for how we interact with and treat those around us. Self-love teaches us to respect our needs and boundaries, and this understanding allows us to respect the needs and boundaries of others. It fosters a sense of empathy and patience, essential qualities for healthy and nurturing relationships.

At the heart of self-love is self-awareness, which helps us recognize our emotions, triggers, and needs. This heightened awareness enables us to take care of ourselves and equips us to better understand and empathize with others. When we are kind and forgiving towards ourselves, we are more likely to extend the same kindness and forgiveness to others, thereby strengthening our relationships. Furthermore, self-love encourages us to be authentic, crucial for building genuine connections with people.

However, it's also important to recognize that practicing self-love is not always easy, especially when faced with personal challenges or stress. Consistent effort is required to maintain a positive self-dialogue and make choices reflecting self-respect and self-care. Yet, these challenges do not diminish the value of self-love; instead, they highlight its importance. By committing to self-love, we enhance our well-being and create a ripple effect that improves our interactions and relationships with others. In essence, the act of loving oneself is intrinsically connected to our ability to love and connect with others.

9. How do I deal with setbacks or relapses in my self-love progress?

Dealing with setbacks or relapses in your self-love progress can be a challenging aspect of the journey toward improved mental and emotional well-being. It is important to recognize that the path to self-love and self-care is rarely linear. There will be moments of high motivation and success, as well as times when old habits or doubts resurface, potentially causing feelings of failure or discouragement. However, these setbacks are not indicators of failure but are instead part of the natural ebb and flow of personal growth. They provide valuable opportunities for learning and deeper self-understanding.

The first step in managing these setbacks is to approach them with kindness and compassion towards oneself. Just as progress is celebrated, struggles should be met with understanding and patience. It's crucial to avoid harsh self-criticism, which can exacerbate feelings of inadequacy. Instead, acknowledge the setback as a normal part of the growth process. This perspective shift allows for a more constructive assessment of what led to the relapse and what can be learned from it. Remember, every setback is a stepping stone toward greater resilience and self-awareness.

Adopting a problem-solving mindset can also be incredibly beneficial. This involves identifying specific challenges that led to the setback and brainstorming practical strategies to overcome them in the future. Whether it's finding new coping mechanisms, adjusting existing self-care practices to be more effective, or seeking additional support from professionals or loved ones, taking proactive steps can empower you to regain control. Setting realistic, incremental goals can also help rebuild confidence and momentum in your self-love practice.

Lastly, it is vital to maintain a support network and reach out when needed. Sharing your experiences, struggles, and insights can not only provide personal relief but also encourage and inspire others who might be facing similar challenges. Encouragement from friends, family, or support groups can bolster your motivation and remind you that you are not alone in your journey. In essence, dealing with setbacks in self-love progress is a multifaceted process involving understanding, acceptance, strategic planning, and supporting a caring community.

10.Why is self-compassion important, and how can I cultivate more of it?

Self-compassion is an essential component of mental and emotional health, fundamentally about treating ourselves with the same kindness, care, and understanding that we would offer to a good friend going through a tough time. It involves recognizing our shared humanity and understanding that suffering and personal failure are part of the universal human experience. Cultivating self-compassion means acknowledging our flaws and mistakes without harsh judgment or criticism, understanding that these do not define our worth or capabilities.

Practicing self-compassion can lead to numerous benefits, including reduced levels of anxiety, depression, and stress. When we approach our experiences with compassion, we are more likely to engage in positive self-talk and less likely to dwell on negative emotions or ruminate on our shortcomings. This shift in perspective enables us to maintain a healthier emotional balance and cope more effectively with challenges and setbacks. Self-compassion fosters resilience, allowing us to bounce back more quickly from difficulties and persist in our goals despite obstacles.

Cultivating more self-compassion can begin with mindfulness exercises that promote an awareness of our thoughts and feelings without judging them. Journaling can help us reflect on our experiences with kindness and understanding. Practicing self-care, such as ensuring enough rest, engaging in physical activity, and connecting with loved ones, can reinforce our commitment to treating ourselves well. Additionally, seeking out compassionate feedback from friends or professionals can provide valuable perspectives and support in cultivating a more compassionate relationship with ourselves. Learning to be empathetic towards ourselves enriches our lives, enhances our relationships with others, and supports our overall well-being.

11. What are the signs that I'm making progress in my self-love journey?

Recognizing progress in your self-love journey can be subtle and vary widely from one person to another. However, several universal signs indicate a positive shift towards greater self-acceptance and care. One of the first signs is a noticeable reduction in self-criticism and an increase in self-compassion. This means you are more forgiving of your mistakes and less likely to engage in negative self-talk. Instead of harshly judging yourself for failures or shortcomings, you understand that mistakes are part of the learning and growth process, and you can treat yourself with kindness and patience.

Another sign of progress is improving your overall mental and emotional well-being. You may feel generally happier, more content, and less prone to anxiety, depression, or stress. This doesn't mean that negative emotions are completely absent, but rather, you are better equipped to manage them healthily. Your resilience in facing challenges and setbacks improves, allowing you to bounce back more quickly and with less emotional turmoil than before. The ability to maintain a positive outlook, even in difficult situations, indicates a strong foundation of self-love.

Additionally, progress in your self-love journey can also manifest through changes in your behaviour and habits. You might notice that you are making healthier choices, setting boundaries, and prioritizing your needs without feeling guilty.

This could include saying no to excessive demands on your time, engaging in self-care practices, and pursuing activities that align with your interests and values. You become more assertive in expressing your needs and desires, demonstrating respect for your own well-being that perhaps wasn't there before.

The signs of progress in the self-love journey are deeply personal and reflect a growing harmony between your mental, emotional, and physical states. They signal a shift towards a more balanced and compassionate self-relationship, marked by an increase in self-compassion, emotional resilience, and proactive self-care. Recognizing these changes in yourself can be incredibly affirming and motivating, reinforcing the importance of continuing on this path of self-improvement and love.

12. How can I remind myself of my worth without coming across as arrogant?

Finding the delicate balance between self-assurance and humility is essential for reminding ourselves of our worth without appearing arrogant. This equilibrium relies on recognizing and appreciating our qualities and achievements while staying grounded in the reality that there is always room for growth and learning. It's about viewing oneself through an honest and appreciative lens that acknowledges both strengths and limitations.

Expressing self-worth healthily involves a genuine

understanding and acceptance of our intrinsic value as human beings, not just for what we achieve but for who we are at our core. It means celebrating our successes and acknowledging our efforts, not belittling others or assuming superiority, but in a way that can inspire both ourselves and those around us. Sharing our achievements with a sense of gratitude and a recognition of the support we've received along the way can help maintain a humble perspective.

Furthermore, self-worth should not only be measured by external success or validation but also by the efforts we put into our personal growth, how we overcome challenges, and how we contribute to the well-being of others. Practicing self-compassion, offering kindness without expecting anything in return, and being open to learning from mistakes are ways to remind ourselves of our worth in a manner that fosters connection rather than separation from others. Cultivating an inner dialogue that supports and acknowledges our value, without comparison to others, fosters a sense of self-worth that is confident yet considerate, thereby avoiding the pitfalls of arrogance.

13. Are there any exercises or activities specifically designed to enhance self-awareness and self-appreciation?

Numerous exercises and activities designed to enhance self-awareness and self-appreciation cater to different preferences and needs. One effective exercise is the practice of daily self-reflection, which involves setting aside a few moments each day to quietly meditate on one's thoughts, emotions, and experiences. This can be done through guided meditation apps, mindful breathing exercises, or simply sitting in silence. The goal is to observe one's inner self without judgment, fostering a deeper understanding of one's own mental and emotional patterns. This practice encourages individuals to confront their true feelings and thoughts, acknowledging them with kindness and without self-criticism, thereby enhancing self-awareness.

Another powerful activity for boosting self-appreciation is gratitude journaling. This involves regularly writing down things one is grateful for about oneself, such as personal strengths, achievements, or positive qualities. This activity shifts focus from what one lacks to the abundance within oneself, facilitating a positive mindset and greater self-appreciation. It serves as a reminder of one's value and contributions, which can often be overlooked in the rush of daily life. Gratitude journaling increases awareness of one's achievements and positive attributes and helps cultivate a more compassionate and forgiving self-view.

In addition to self-reflection and gratitude journaling, engaging in self-kindness is another vital exercise in enhancing self-awareness and self-appreciation. This could range from treating oneself to a favourite activity, dedicating time to pursue a hobby or interest, or simply allowing time to rest and recuperate. These acts of kindness towards oneself reinforce the notion of self-worth and the importance of caring for one's well-being. They remind individuals that they deserve love and respect, starting from within. This, in turn, builds a healthier relationship with oneself, characterized by appreciation and acknowledgment of one's needs and desires.

Together, these exercises serve as practical tools for individuals to enhance their self-awareness and cultivate deeper self-appreciation. By regularly practicing these activities, individuals can develop a stronger, more compassionate relationship with themselves, which is crucial for overall mental and emotional well-being. Through this ongoing process, people learn to value themselves not just for achievements or based on external validation but for their inherent worth as individuals. This fosters a resilient and positive self-image that is essential for navigating life's challenges with confidence and grace.

14. How can I differentiate between self-love and selfishness?

Self-love and selfishness often get conflated, but they stand on fundamentally different grounds. Self-love is about recognizing and valuing one's worth, prioritizing self-care, and making decisions that foster growth, health, and well-being. It is an act of self-respect that enables individuals to thrive, contributing to their ability to support and care for others effectively. Self-love involves setting healthy boundaries, practicing self-compassion, and engaging in activities that nourish the body, mind, and spirit. It's about being kind to oneself, forgiving oneself for past mistakes, and acknowledging one's needs and feelings without judgment.

Selfishness, on the other hand, implies a disregard for others' needs and feelings, prioritizing one's desires and benefits at the expense of others. It often stems from fear, insecurity, or a lack of empathy, leading individuals to act in ways that serve their interests without considering the impact on those around them. Selfish behaviour can damage relationships, create conflicts, and foster a toxic atmosphere in personal circles or broader communities. It contrasts with self-love, which enhances an individual's capacity for empathy, understanding, and generosity by ensuring they are psychologically and emotionally balanced.

Understanding the distinction between self-love and selfishness is crucial for personal development and maintaining healthy relationships. Practicing self-love allows for a more authentic life and deepens connections with others because it comes from a place of abundance and security. When individuals care for themselves and acknowledge their worth, they are less likely to act out of insecurity or neediness, often the roots of selfish actions. Self-love fosters a sense of inner security and abundance, which encourages generosity and a desire to support others, demonstrating that truly loving oneself expands the capacity to love and care for others rather than detracting from

15.What role does forgiveness (of self and others) play in the self-love process?

Forgiveness, both of oneself and others is a pivotal aspect of the self-love process. It involves releasing resentment, anger or wishes for retribution that may linger after you or someone else has made a mistake or acted poorly. For self-love, forgiving oneself is crucial because it allows individuals to move past their errors and imperfections, recognizing that these do not define their worth or capabilities. It means acknowledging that everyone makes mistakes, and these moments are opportunities for growth and learning rather than reasons for self-punishment or harsh criticism. This aspect of self-love paves the way for personal development, as it encourages individuals to accept their humanity and work towards self-improvement with kindness and understanding.

Similarly, forgiving others is essential in letting go of negative emotions that may bind us to past events, freeing ourselves from ongoing mental and emotional discomfort. Holding onto grudges or resentment can consume a significant amount of emotional energy and space in one's mind, which could be redirected towards more positive and self-affirming thoughts and actions. Forgiveness towards others also reflects a profound understanding of human fallibility and the complexity of human behaviour, acknowledging that people's actions are often influenced by their circumstances, pains, or limited perspectives. It is not about condoning wrongful acts but rather about choosing to release oneself from the additional burden that holding onto resentment brings.

Furthermore, practicing forgiveness is deeply intertwined with cultivating empathy and compassion towards oneself and others. It requires a sincere effort to see beyond the surface of our actions and those of others, striving to understand the underlying factors that led to those actions. This compassionate stance fosters a sense of common humanity, reducing feelings of isolation and enhancing connections with others. By integrating forgiveness into the self-love process, individuals can work towards building a life characterized by emotional freedom, resilience, and more meaningful relationships. This leads to a healthier state of mind and a more fulfilling life, as it aligns with the principles of self-respect and self-worth that are fundamental to self-love.

Thank You

Thank you sincerely for taking the time to explore this journey through the pages of our book. Your commitment to personal growth and self-understanding is commendable.

We hope the insights shared have fostered a deeper self-awareness and inspired actionable steps toward nurturing self-love and cultivating healthier relationships in your life. Remember, the path to self-improvement is ongoing and uniquely yours. May you continue to move forward with grace, resilience, and an open heart, creating a life filled with purpose, joy, and fulfilment.

Your dedication to this process enriches not only your own life but also those around you. Carry forward this spirit of mindfulness and compassion, and watch the world transform with you.

Made in the USA
Las Vegas, NV
12 December 2024

13939811R00132